The Royal Palace Gardens

&
History of Raikes Hall

David Slattery-Christy

Incorporating some original Research by

Alan Seddon

Copyright © 2016 David Slattery-Christy

All rights reserved.

ISBN-10: 153015491X
ISBN-13: 978-1530154913

GRATEFUL THANKS TO

Everyone who has helped with information and images of the
Gardens included in this book.

The Royal Archives, Windsor Castle.
Pamela Clark, Peter Jackson, Shirley Burrows, Elaine Martin, Aileesh
Evans, Alan Seddon, Graham Greenwood, Dave Blacker MBE,
Robert Smith Literary Agent, Music Hall Guild of Great Britain & America,
Adrian Barry, Matthew Neil, Richard Baker, Shirley Evans,
Ron Howard, Beverly & Keith Walsh, Matthew Lloyd
Johnston Press Ltd, Dominique Jando at Circopedia,
Arthur Lloyd www.arthurlloyd.co.uk

Thanks also to Tom Marshall for colourising
the cover image for this book.
http://www.photogra-fix.com/

PhotograFix
Professional Photo Restoration

Wreckers often lured unsuspecting ships to their doom so they could plunder their rich cargos. William Butcher of Raikes Hall had such a reputation.

CHAPTERS

	Acknowledgments	i
	Author's Note	1
	Foreword by David Blacker MBE	5
	Introduction	7
1	Prince of Shipwrecks & Early Days	11
2	Sisters of The Holy Child Jesus	15
3	Victorian Pleasure Opportunities	29
4	Music Hall & Variety Artistes Extraordinaire!	45
5	Competing Attractions	59
6	Troubled Times – The Show Must Go On!	69
7	Botanical Legacy & Royal Titles	77
8	Progress & Founders Early Death	87
9	Let There Be Electric Illumination!	91
10	Entertainment Rivals	97
11	Royal Palace Gardens for Sale	105
12	The Final Curtain	115
	References	132
	Further Reading – Circus & Shows	132
	Artist Biographies & Details	134

ACKNOWLEDGMENTS

Special thanks to my friend and collaborator, **Alan Seddon**, for generously allowing me to use some of his initial research into the Raikes Hall history for this book. It would have been impossible without him and his excellent knowledge of local history.

Also special thanks to **Ed Christiano** at **Deeper Blue Designs** for brilliant cover designs for this book. www.wearedeeperblue.co.uk

Special thanks to the **Music Hall Guild of Great Britain & America** for helping with information and biographies of some of the artistes that appeared at the Gardens between 1872 and 1901 – especially founder Adrian Barry and Matthew Neil. The charity does extraordinary and important work to ensure the legacy of Music Hall and Variety artistes live on for future generations. Please support them.

www.themusichallguild.com
Registered Charity: 1014674

Author's Note

Some years ago, when going through the old paper deeds for the house I live in on Whitegate Drive [once Whitegate Lane], I was intrigued by the map and reference to the Royal Place Gardens that the house once overlooked when it was built in Victorian Villa style in 1893. Further investigation uncovered this lost Victorian Pleasure Gardens and its scope and scale was incredible and a real revelation to me. More astounding was the fact that in 1901 it closed and was torn down and the land sold off as building plots. The only survivor was the original Georgian Hall that first occupied the site – Raikes Hall. That building still sits amongst the houses and serves as a public house today.

More recently I was given a booklet of the research carried out by local historian Alan Seddon into the history of this part of Blackpool's rich past. I am grateful that Alan has allowed me to use his research and enhance it with my own to create this book. His passion for the history inspired me to delve deeper. It was then it occurred to me that this wonderful pleasure garden and its history, and that of Raikes Hall, had to be preserved for posterity and thus I decided to create this book to that aim. From its very beginnings to the present day it has been a history full of intrigue and msytery. From private residence to a convent, and then to the Victorian's ultimate entertainment venue, the estate has come a long way. I did not want this book to be an academic study, but a light and easy read and a joyful journey to the past.

Initially the Gardens were known as the Raikes Hall Gardens and it was in 1887, to commemorate Queen Victoria's Golden Jubilee, that the Gardens changed its name to the Royal Palace Gardens. For purposes of ease and to prevent confusion for the reader I will refer to them as the 'Gardens' or 'Royal Palace Gardens' rather than switch betwixt the names.

As a child I first experienced the vibrance and thrill of Blackpool during the 1960s when my mother first bought a hotel in the resort. Little did I realise that I was actually living through the end of an era. As the popularity of the resort waned, as cheaper foreign holidays took over, it was sad to see the decline – indeed it still is. But on a more positive note, the iconic buildings in the town have been given listed status, and have finally been restored, or are undergoing restoration, to their former glories, and other venues like the

Regent Cinema, so nearly lost has been saved through private investment. The Raikes Hall, and its surrounding streets, have now become the Raikes Hall Conservation Area to protect its heritage and listed buildings, plus those built by the fabulous Victorians, and those built on land that was once part of the Royal Palace Gardens. Fantastic and positive moves to protect the town's heritage – sadly we still lose iconic buildings to demolition. Latterly the ABC Theatre, originally built in 1894 as the Hippodrome Theatre. It should never happen that such history is disregarded by any town, never mind a town as rich in entertainment and theatre history as Blackpool.

On completing this book, I feel that I have given back something to Blackpool. It is my way of saying thank you. Now I can close my eyes and I can walk through the imposing main gates, pay my sixpence entrance fee, and walk down through the manicured drive and gardens, past the boating lake and the sports grounds, and see the Indian Pavilion, Ballroom and the Grand Opera House in all their glory. The fountains dance and the Italian Gardens enchant as grand couples go by in their horse and carriages to enjoy the view and marvel at the Grecian statues posing on their pedestals. The heat of the conservatory envelopes me as I walk past the smiling concierge, the ferns and the waterfalls create a magical, humid atmosphere. In the distance I can hear the shrieks of pleasure and laughter from the roller skating rink next door. The sound of the monkeys chanting and screeching in play, and the tropical birds cawing from the aviary. Sitting on the bench, the gardeners go by, engrossed and proud of their work, they smile cheerily. Closing my eyes I cannot imagine a finer way to spend some time than at the Royal Palace Gardens, Blackpool. I hope you can join me.

David Slattery-Christy M.A.
September 2016

First published by Christyplays Books, 2016
Disributed via Amazon Createspace an independent publishing platform.
www.christyplays.co.uk
email: slatterychristy@aol.co.uk

For distributor details and how to order see Amazon or email the above for further details.

Copyright : The rights of David Slattery-Christy as author has been asserted in accordance with the Copyright, Designs and Patents Act 1988

A CIP catalogue record for this book is available
From the British Library

Design : Christyplays
Book cover designed by Ed Christiano at
Deeper Blue Designs
www.db-md.co.uk

Main Entrance – Church Street at junction with Park Road

Carriage Drive at Royal Palace Gardens. Circa 1890.

Foreword

These days a lot is talked about Communities benefiting from past efforts and historical insights. For example the enormous amounts of cash plowed into supporting our Rio Olympic athletes designed to create a positive 'sporting Legacy' for future generations.

However, it is far harder to gain a 'Positive Community Legacy' from past local history if little is known about them.

Much is known about Blackpool's town centre Heritage but little up to now has been understood about the vital part played by areas like ours in making Blackpool a major seaside destination. Exactly why this gap in our local historical picture exists is a mystery, which may never be solved. Although, this book will help to put the pieces of the jigsaw together.

Thanks to the efforts of a few dedicated individuals, and an important book like this one, things have begun to change for those, like myself, who live within the newly designated Raikes Hall Conservation Area.

Since Talbot Ward fell under the Conservation area, things have begun to change for the better. The tearing down and wanton destruction or alteration of beautiful buildings now has to be stringently vetted by our Council's planning department. Trees and grassy areas are also now protected from irresponsible destruction.

Perhaps more importantly local people now feel that they have an opportunity to create their own 'Positive Legacy' based on newly discovered past glories, but very much looking towards the future. For example there is currently a move to create a new strawberry growing Community Garden, historically reflecting our past.

David's book should go some way in providing a comprehensive insight for anyone interested in local history and an inspirational starting point for those wishing to help create a positive legacy with historical roots.
After all, as Winston Churchill once said **"A nation which has forgotten its past can have no future"**, this we hold as true for our local community.

Dave Blacker MBE
September 2016

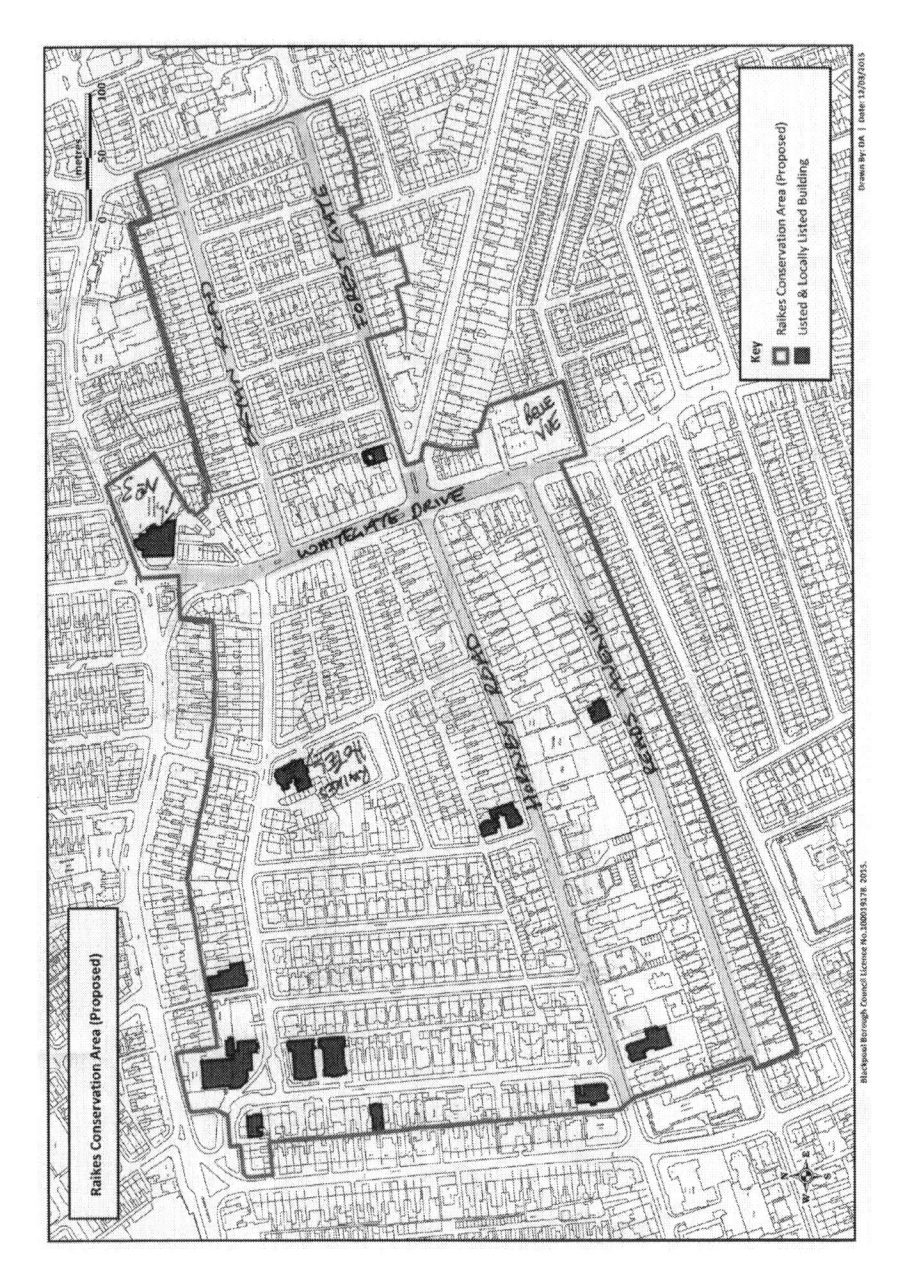

History of Raikes Hall

Raikes Hall Conservation Area Map

Introduction

Through three centuries the Raikes Hall has remained something of an enigma. Consistent local rumour has been entwined with fact and woven with a kaleidoscope of intrigue. Yet for almost three decades in Victorian England, Blackpool's much neglected Raikes Hall Estate captured the hearts and memories of Blackpool's visitors. Its popularity was such that it was comparable to the world famous Tivoli Gardens in Copenhagen. Indeed, ironically, that popularity was in part responsible for its eventual decline and demise – the famous Gardens that bore a royal title slipped into ruin and the land eventually sold off and replaced with housing and streets that remain to this day. But why? Why was this preeminent visitor attraction that predated the Tower, the Winter Gardens and two of the famous piers allowed to vanish as if it never existed? The man so capable of building success, John Bickerstaffe, the man behind the construction of the Tower, Winter Gardens and Piers, seemed to lose his magic touch when it came to the Royal Palace Gardens at Raikes Hall. Or perhaps, once he established himself as a director on the board, he was able to slowly undermine the major attraction that took important visitors away from spending their money in his new Winter Garden and Tower attractions? Whatever the truth behind this, the Royal Palace Gardens were closed down by 1901. All that survived was the original Georgian Hall, that is now still popular as the Raikes Public House. Many of those who live in the houses and streets surrounding it know little of the history and almost unbelievable spectacles that were enacted in the Gardens. The ghosts of that past still vibrant and strong today – if you allow them to come alive in your imagination.

This book is intended to give you an understanding of the strange, exciting and often turbulent history that formed these unique and grand Victorian Pleasure Gardens, now largely forgotten in Blackpool's recorded history. A history that seems to focus on the resort from the time the Tower was built in 1894. It has been a real surprise for local people today to learn of what once existed in what has now become the new Raikes Hall Conservation Area.

Within this book it is also intended to put to rest some of the more outlandish rumours and speculation regarding the short period the religious order of Catholic nuns occupied the Raikes Hall until it was sold to create the pleasure Gardens in the mid 19th century. That devout female religious order, who eventually moved to Layton to build a convent on a hill, ran it as a school. More of that later, as it was felt a chapter was needed to explore that brief but unique part of Raikes Hall's history.

The original Raikes Hall was built as a seaside retreat in 1750 by the infamous profiteer William Bucher – pronounced and written as 'Butcher' by locals over time. That is how I shall refer to him in this book. Some years after Butcher's demise in 1769, the estate was acquired by the fashionable Hornby Family. The local visionaries who purchased the estate from the Hornby's introduced the ideal ingredients for success – innovation and enterprise! They changed the 40 acre estate into a veritable haven of pleasure that the previous occupants would certainly have frowned upon! In time thousands would stream through the gates paying their entrance fee of sixpence – not an inconsiderable sum at the time – coining the Raikes' advertising phrase:

"Nowhere in the world can so much be seen for so little!"

It would certainly live up to that statement – in spades!

The Victorian Villas on Whitegate Drive between Bryan Road and Forest Gate were completed in 1893. Their raised elevations would have given them views across the Royal Palace Gardens at the height of their popularity. These houses are the only ones that survived from that era – along with the Belle Vue and the Number 3 on Whitegate Drive.

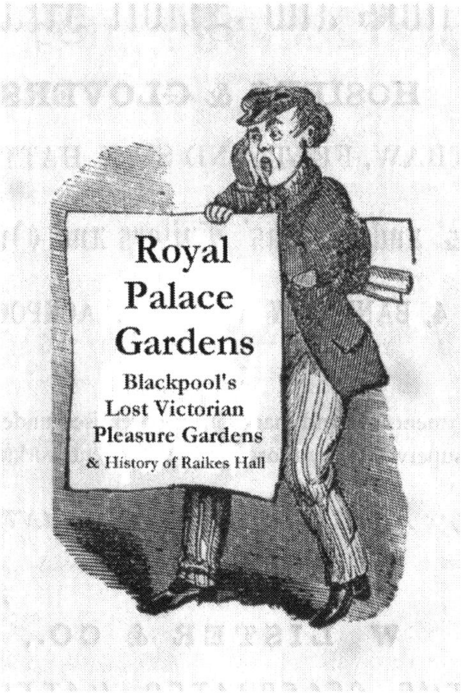
Royal
Palace
Gardens
Blackpool's
Lost Victorian
Pleasure Gardens
& History of Raikes Hall

Chapter 1

PRINCE OF SHIPWRECKS & EARLY DAYS

During the latter decades of Victoria's reign, the public's insatiable demand for entertainment and recreational extraordinaire was arguably at its height, and for almost three decades Blackpool's Raikes Hall and the Royal Palace Gardens catered for this 19th century phenomena. Yet through the passage of time, and a will by some to erase it from the town's history, this Mecca of pleasure is sadly no more – and worse – so little remembered today. This reason alone is why it is important to record for posterity that lost era's shining example of populist leisure for the masses. It had no equal in the days before the Tower and Winter Gardens were built. Even the early piers struggled to be more popular than the Royal Palace Gardens. Had it survived in its entirety, it would surely be a world heritage site and protected from demolition. But sadly, all that physically remains of its former architectural glory is Butcher's original home, now the Raikes Public House, and its adjacent green oasis – the bowling green, once the land that supported the Garden's grand Indian Pavilion – a tiny pocket of land that is a mere postage stamp in size to what did surround that once magnificent Georgian Hall.

The original Raikes Hall can be traced back to the middle of the 18th Century. Local evangelical chronicler, William Thornber, influenced historical thought by his documented comments made some years ago. Thornber believed that a certain Kirkham man, Willian Butcher, built his imposing seaside retreat, that he called Raikes Hall, from the illicit proceeds of ship wrecking.

Seemingly, during this mid 18th century period, Butcher belonged to an infamous breed of men who were common enough along these coastal waters. They were land based profiteers or freebooters generally known as ship-wreckers who relieved floundering merchant vessels of their valuable cargoes and were not averse to deliberately setting up false lights on cliff or shore to deliberately beach unwary vessels. True or not, Butcher built his Raikes Hall circa. 1750. His wealth provided a mansion surrounded by an estate and grounds of character.

Kathleen Eyre's wonderful book on Blackpool's history titled Seven Golden Miles has this interesting inclusion on Butcher and his Raikes Hall:

"Originally a gentleman's residence of considerable dignity, set in the midst of a large, tree-girt, and beautifully maintained estate. Raikes Hall, a Georgian house, was built by Mr. Butcher who, according to Vicar Thornber and the gossip ripe in his day, [that Butcher] had sprung from obscurity to wealth by somewhat dubious means. Mid-eighteenth century Blackpudlians, astonished no doubt by this grandiose building operation, put their own…construction upon the situation. Who, for instance, had not noticed Mr. Butcher's frequent trips to the seashore? And wasn't it odd, to say the least of it, that Raikes Hall was commissioned shortly after a vessel containing the riches of three sisters had been cast up on the coast – especially as the reputed 'treasure' had never come to light? Sourly, and not without envy, it was whispered that Mr. Butcher must have got there first."

The coastline at Gynn when ships were in danger from the rocks.

Whatever the truth, Butcher ruled his forty-acre domain with the enthusiasm and manner of a country squire. His trappings of wealth were there to enjoy, in particular his interest in the 'Sport of Kings' – horse racing. He stabled his valuable steeds near the old Foxhall. The broad expanse of Blackpool's sandy beaches became the exercise yard for them. This part of his pleasure was but a short ride away and he could race and entertain his friends in the exhilarating atmosphere near the sea – no doubt the dangers sometimes involved during squally and stormy weather adding to the thrill of the chase. These equestrian pleasures no doubt helped him to continue his business dealings and helped to elevate his status within the wider communities. Not exactly a pirate in the true sense of the word, but nonetheless his dealings with wrecked ships and vanishing cargos gave him an enigmatic, and perhaps slightly fearful reputation among many of his contemporaries.

Butcher reigned at his beloved Raikes Hall for about two decades. As he stood at his first floor drawing room and looked from the large windows surveying the panoramic view of his estate, he could not have guessed the journey the hall and the vast grounds would take in the future – a future he was not destined to see. Certainly he would have been dazzled at what would be created in the grounds and surely pleased that his beloved Raikes Hall would remain at its heart little unchanged on the exterior; indeed he would marvel that the hall would still be standing proudly, if at times somewhat forlornly, nearly 270 years after it was built. Laughing heartily no doubt, that sometime in between it had even been a convent for nuns! His death in 1769 at the age of eighty five brought to an end his era of mystery and intrigue. He took the secrets about the source of his wealth to his grave. Interred in a Bispham graveyard, his epitaph reads:

"His pleasures were to give or lend, he always stood a poor man's friend."

Although he had appeared to the locals as a sinister character, he was in fact something of a Robin Hood figure and many of Blackpool's poor and misfortunates benefited from his generous handouts. A rogue perhaps by profession and yet a philanthropist by nature. Incidentally, and surely by no coincidence, the name Raikes is derived from the word wreckers – wraikes – raikes! There was also a popular term used at the time – a raikes progress. Being referred to as a "bit of a raike" was both a compliment and an insult depending on how one chose to interpret it. Usually the so named was different, a chancer, took risks in life, or crossed boundaries of decency or morality of the time. Whatever, being a raike was, for some, like Butcher, a badge of honour that set him apart from ordinary men. That suited him just fine. An eccentric would perhaps be another name to attach to him.

After Butcher's death his son William inherited Raikes Hall. He and his close relatives remained the Lords of the Manor until 1820 when, due to financial circumstances, they sold the estate. William Hornby became the proud owner of Raikes Hall and the entire estate and grounds.

The Hornby's were an upper middle class family, products of the Georgian period where taste and an appreciation of elegance and current fashions was a reflection of their standing in the wider community. Their innovation and drive, along with their money, meant that no expense was spared in refurbishing Raikes Hall – the visual embodiment of their values and aspirations. A fine status symbol that established their supremacy in the area, and on the community at that time. One of the Hornby ladies introduced the very first carpets to Blackpool, having them specially woven and fitted in the many rooms of their new home. The Raikes Hall became a symbol of prosperity and respectability in their hands, instead of the shady and secretive reputation it garnered under its previous ownership. That said, the legend of Butcher and his dark past were still whispered in the local community and stories about him persisted like a ghost haunting the corridors and grounds of his former home. As it happens, his would not be the only ghost to haunt the Raikes Hall in years to come, he would be joined by a nun and a small child.

The head of the Hornby family, William, died in 1824 whereupon ownership passed to his brother, John, who up until then had lived in Blackburn. John spent 17 years at Raikes Hall until his death in 1841 when it passed to his son, Daniel. An eccentric character, Daniel finally sold Raikes Hall in 1870. It would seem that the cost of the upkeep and maintenance for such a large house and the extensive grounds just made it impossible financially. His solution initially was to rent it out. New tenants were installed by 1860.

Chapter 2

SISTERS OF THE HOLY CHILD JESUS

In 1859/60 the Raikes welcomed its new tenants 'The Sisters of the Holy Child Jesus', a devout Catholic order who ran a strict girls convent school from the Hall. Rumours of mysterious underground tunnels to connect the Raikes with a nearby male religious order at Layton have persisted to the present day – the notion of clandestine meetings betwixt the occupants delighting gossips of the day. Some years ago, much to everyone's surprise, whilst undertaking work in the cellar of the Raikes Public House, a tunnel was discovered extending several yards towards Layton but alas, due to the collapsed walls bringing it to an abrupt end, it's ultimate destination will remain a mystery forever.

The period the Nuns ran the Convent School at Raikes Hall is an interesting interlude in the history and as such is worth documenting for this study. The first residence of the convent school was in fact a little nearer to the centre of Blackpool, and the sea front, at Queen Street or Queen's Sqaure. The instigator and founder for the order to establish a Convent School at Blackpool was Mother Cornelia Connelly, who was determined to sow the seeds of an order in new soil after it crumbled in its original home of Liverpool. This new first home in Blackpool was remembered in the school's official history:

"In 1856 the first sisters arrived and 'were received with great kindness by the Misses Cookson [the Misses Cookson were sisters of Provost Cookson of Liverpool and of Mr. Richard Cookson who owned Layton House outside Blackpool which had its own chapel] who gave them shelter in their house until they could move into the small house in Queen's Square which they rented for three years.' This house backed onto Talbot Square a few yards from the Jesuit Church, which they had opened in 1857. Alphonsa Kay was the first superior and she brought with her four sisters and twelve boarders. It was noted that 'Mother Teresa Hanson was sent by [Mother] Cornelia to be the head mistress.' School began at once in the large back room where children were seated on rough wooden benches arranged in tiers. Alice Thornton, whose three older sisters were sent at this time to Queen's Square, noted that 'all went to Mass in a cellar-room in the inn.' The inn in question was later the Railway Hotel. The Talbot Road poor school was [also] held in this cellar room."

This first home would last them for barely four years and because of the restrictions it imposed upon them due to its small size, and the desire to expand the school and create something more permanent, Mother Cornelia started to look around for alternative accommodation for the Convent School. There were other reasons perhaps why a move further inland was seen as appropriate. The popularity of Blackpool and its promenade and pleasures were developing fast and thus a little too close to home for the Sisters – the distractions they created for their charges not suitable or appropriate for young impressionable girls in their care. It was obvious the growing tourist trade and the temptations that brought would only get worse.

The history records note that Blackpool "was growing fast" stating that "in 1863 the Central [train] Station was opened, in 1868 the Central Pier and in 1869 the [complete] Promenade." In addition the school had grown and changed with "numbers in the Queen's Square school rising to 21 and new accommodation was urgently needed."

The choices in a relatively new town were limited, unless Mother Cornelia could secure the finances to actually build their own school. This being out of the question at this time, although still part of her long-term ambition, she decided to scour the outlying neighborhoods for suitable premises. She had seen an advert in the local press and wondered if at last a suitable new home might be possible.

It was described thus in the local newspaper:

'TO BE LET, for term of years, furnished or unfurnished, a very compact and convenient FAMILY MANSION, known by the name of 'RAIKES HALL', containing on the ground floor, Dining-room, Breakfast-room, and entrance hall; on the first floor, large Drawing-room, four Bed-rooms and Dressing-room, Bath-room, and Water-closet; the upper storey contains four [servant] Bed-rooms.

THE Domestic apartments contain Butler's Pantry, Servants' Hall, Sewing-room, Kitchens, Sculleries, Pantries, Wash-house, Laundry, Boot-house, &c, and five Bed-rooms, Wine and Beer Cellars. The outbuildings consist of Coach-house, two-stalled Stables, Loose Boxes and Saddle-room, Paddock, &c [water closet]]..

THE Gardens are walled in, and are in excellent order, and well stocked with Choice Fruit Trees. RAIKES HALL is about five minutes' walk from the Church [St John's], and fifteen minutes' walk from Blackpool and the [North] Railway Station. [Further] land may be had if required.

Apply to JAMES CARR, 103, Fishergate, Preston."

Mother Cornelia was quick to apply. It seemed to offer the ideal solution and had land and all the space that was required to establish a larger and more productive Convent School – more importantly – one that was well away from the hustle and bustle of the centre of Blackpool and its temptations to their young charges. However, she felt that it was only right to seek out the opinion of the Bishop to make sure he approved and more importantly supported her intentions. It is interesting to wonder if she had any idea of the Raikes Hall's history and the foundations on which it was built by Butcher's ill-gotten gains and his less than salubrious reputation. If so, it seems not to have deterred her from her mission. Setting pen to paper, Mother Cornelia sent this letter to Bishop Goss of Liverpool on the 6th August 1859:

"I hope I shall not be troublesome in so soon again writing to your Lordship, but in the present instance we require your advice and direction. Our Sisters at Blackpool have now the opportunity of renting Raikes Hall, which is a much more commodious dwelling and more suitable for a Convent than the house they now occupy, offering abundant accommodation for their Schools at a rent of about £50 pr. Annum more than the present rent. The walk from the Church [Sacred Heart on Talbot

Road] would be about ten to twenty minutes. We unanimously think the change would be most desirable & (sic) even necessary for the success of the Schools, and in fact the difference of the rent would be more than made up by the advantage of accommodation & (sic) position. Mr. Hornby is willing to give us a lease of 7 years. Will your Lordship kindly say whether you approve of this change as soon as convenient, as our Sisters are afraid the old gentleman may change his mind & (sic) that they may thus be held back another year."

Cornelia Connelly in 1874

She need not have worried, the Bishop was quick to respond and give his blessing to Mother Cornelia taking the lease on Raikes Hall on behalf of the order. No doubt he would have seen the obvious benefits of having more room and space in the grounds and that overall it was a much more suitable place to establish the Convent School for young girls – and indeed the Sisters who would live and teach there. Mother Mary Ignatia Bridges was also excited at the prospect of the new home and recorded in her diary from December 1859 the day that the Raikes received the ultimate blessing for its future use.

"The Blessed Sacrament was brought there on December 3rd and placed in the [new] chapel & the house was blessed. Holy Mass was said there for the first time on the feast of St Thomas of Canterbury [29th December] & about once a week from this date until Sept 9th 1860; then Father de Pietro S.J. being appointed as Chaplain, said daily Mass & performed the usual services."

Raikes Hall during the time it was a Convent School in the 1860s.
The woods and grounds clearly visible. [Picture with thanks to Peter Jackson.] The new wing to the right of the Hall was added during the time of the Royal Palace Gardens years later Circa. 1890s

The Sisters quickly established the school and their community and the grounds allowed them a good deal of self sufficiency as they could grow their own supplies and have animals suitable for a small holding to provide eggs and milk. This was an added bonus for the Sisters and allowed them a greater sense of freedom and also the pleasures of living in a more rural environment – certainly a world away from the busy urban bustle that they had lived amongst in Queen's Square. However, in spite of moving away they did not forget the poor school that was held at the Talbot Hotel. For a period of time two Sisters would continue to travel into Queen Street at least once a week to continue to teach the poor children.

Mother Cornelia Connolly is also a character full of surprises and her life history was certainly not what one would expect to find. She was born in the United States of America and her family were prominent in the Philadelphia community. Cornelia Peacock was born in 1809 and was the youngest child – she had six siblings. Her parents were proud of their ancestry which gave them direct links back to Yorkshire in the United Kingdom. In 1831 she met and married a fellow Catholic convert, and curate, Pierce Connelly. They went on to have five children. A girl child died at less than two months old, a boy was scolded by boiling marmalade and died from the burns aged two and a half. Her two daughters became nuns and her son lived an errant life after being schooled at Stoneyhurst College in Lancashire.

A few years after their marriage, they lived and worked at a convent and also traveled to Europe as guests of the Catholic Lord Shrewsbury from Alton Towers. Returning to the United States, they took up residence again in a convent near Mississippi. It was here that Pierce went on a four day retreat with the Jesuit priests and returned to tell Cornelia that from that point they would live as brother and sister because he wanted to be a priest. Dispensation had been sought from Rome. Cornelia was devastated but accepted what her husband told her whilst also wondering if this was God's way to bring her into the fold. She had worked closely with the nuns and began to find that the life they led suited her spiritual and emotional needs. She wanted to emulate their kindness and their good works.

Pierce Connolly was asked to travel to Rome to put his case before the Cardinals. His being married made the request all the more unusual but not impossible to grant. He had his audience and was even given a brief meeting with the Pope. The Cardinals decided that before they could grant any request, they needed to speak to Cornelia. Pierce hurriedly arranged this meeting and date was set a few months hence. He traveled back to the United States to collect Cornelia and the surviving children apart from their eldest daughter who wanted to remain at the convent as she was taking holy orders herself. Piers returned to Rome with Cornelia. She had asked him one last time if he was certain he wanted to denounce their marriage and become a priest. He declined. His mind was made up and there was no going back. As much as she loved him and understood, there was a part of her that was heartbroken. Again she drew on her faith and nearness to God to allow her to accept and support his choice to be ordained. On meeting the Cardinals in Rome they were impressed by the devotion they both showed to God. Permission was granted, they decreed, as long as Cornelia gave her permission and would also take a vow of chastity. This she readily agreed. This is how Mother Cornelia Connelly became a nun, and why she decided to create the Order of the Holy Child Jesus to educate young girls in the Catholic Faith. Cornelia wrote in her notebook reproduced in her biography A Study in Fidelity by Mother Maria Theresa:

"He who putteth his hand to the plough and looketh back is not fit for the Kingdom of Heaven. Many are called, but few are chosen."

She believed she had been called. From this point on Mother Cornelia's very being was embedded in the schools she established for young girls. She came to her calling and took her vows after so much life experience and being a mother herself. She was certainly a woman of great kindness, wisdom and determination. She would live the rest of her life in England devoting herself completely to God's work. Moving the convent school to Raikes Hall was just part of a longer term plan perhaps. She always put her faith in God to do whatever was needed to help her.

A former pupil, Alice Thornton, recalled her experiences at the Raikes Hall Convent and how, with much irony, it was actually one of the founding Sisters who established the theatrical seed in the grounds of the hall.

"I went to the Raikes as a pupil when my elder sister left in 1861 and was there 7 years. The Raikes was an old house with farmyard & barn etc adjoining the house and situated in its own grounds consisting of 2 woods, one small one containing laburnum trees near the house & a larger one further away [and] several fields. Thus as there were very few buildings between the Raikes and the sea, in those days the house was rather isolated. Mother Theresa came from Queen's Square [under directions of Mother Cornelia] and started the foundation [school] with 21 girls but when I went in [September] 1861 Mother Theresa had left to become [a] Mother Foundress' Assistant & Mother Gertrude was then Reverent Mother.

"Life at the Raikes was the same as most big schools, but as there were no public exams in those days we had more holidays, the big feasts and nuns' feasts being kept specially. We did not go home except for the six weeks at Midsummer. At Christmas we had a fortnights holiday spent at the Convent and were allowed Christmas Boxes, their arrival and unpacking causing a good deal of excitement. Being rather delicate I used to [sometime have to] go home for the Christmas holidays & remember well helping mother to pack the boxes sent to my [friends at the Convent]. On the nuns' feasts and holidays, especially in the summer, we used to go for picnics to Cleveleys, or Norbreck.

"Also in the summer from about June till the breaking up in July, the bigger girls went down at 6.30am to bathe in the sea & be taught swimming etc; one half of the girls going one day & the rest on the next, all having a bite of bread while dressing in the vans [bathing vans were commonly used for modesty and privacy for women and men in the Victorian period] before returning. One special day was a holiday given on account of our number reaching 50. That day we spent at Cleveleys and had great fun there. On Rev. Mother's Feast…we had three days holiday & usually acted a play at that time, among those I remember [was] Hamlet, The Merchant of Venice, & a French Play [no doubt a French Farce popular at that time as much for learning the language as for their hilarity!]."

The Convent was quickly established and the school thrived. It is good to hear that the girls who boarded were generally content and enjoyed some happy times and fun in spite of the hard work expected during lessons and, it has to be said, the rather modest and Spartan accommodations quite usual at the time. Mother Cornelia was sent a report as to the progress of the Raikes in circa. 1860 by the Sisters who delightedly announced that:

"On Christmas Eve we had Midnight Mass at the Convent for the first time. [We] have been free from all persecutions and contradictions [by those in the community] and generally much esteemed by those who have dealings with us. The amount of donations from Externs [those from the wider community] received during the year [is] £176. 4s. 2d."

That was quite a considerable sum of money for the time. That said, there were those who could see the benefits of a rigorous education for girls and were willing to help by donations. The Catholic Directory of circa. 1860 set out the educational ethos of the Convent:

"Convent of the Holy Child Jesus, Raikes Square, Blackpool. The Sisters of the Society of the Holy Child Jesus, from St Leonard's-on-sea, conduct a Boarding-school for Young Ladies at their Convent in Blackpool, where the benefit of a sound religious and mental training is combined with the physical advantage of the pure invigorating air of a sea-side residence. The course of studies comprises all the usual branches of English instruction, in which Latin, French, and Drawing are included. German, Italian, and Music, are extras. The pension [Fee per child] is £28 per annum. Any minor details [health issues, special needs, or other problems with the proposed child] should be supplied on application to the Superioress. References may be made to the Rev. George Bampton, S.J."

The theatrical seeds of the future were firmly established by Mother Cornelia, albeit unwittingly, as recalled by another pupil who herself took religious orders in later life, Mother Mary Wenceslaus Higgins. This glimpse of life at the Convent she drew from a memoir of a pupil now anonymous because of lost records:

"[The] uniform [was] 'a dress made as far as possible according to the fashion of the day. The colour was changed to grey, then brown, then blue every three years.' It was made at the school at a cost of 12 shillings and in addition each child had to bring two pairs of sheets, three pillow cases, six towels, six table napkins, a knife, silver fork, spoon and goblet. Outdoor games at the Raikes Convent were Camp, Bataille, Burnt Ball [now called Rounders] and rides on a piebald pony. There was a wonderful barn and Mother Connelly had this fitted out with a stage as she felt that drama was a very important part of education. This barn also contained a swing and according to Mother Wenceslaus this was not allowed to go very high as the ground was cobblestoned and a fall would have been dangerous."

It would appear that the Convent school at Raikes Hall was far from being a poor or charity establishment – at least going on the items the girl's families were required to provide and of course the annual fee for attending the school. There were many wealthy and middle-class catholic families who were delighted to send their young girls to such a school to give them an education that would ultimately either enhance their marriage opportunities or inspire them to take holy orders themselves and perhaps even go on to teach in similar Convent Schools.

By 1865 there were other pressing matters to consider and attend to. The first being the fact that the original lease they had taken out was due to expire in 1866. The lease would be extended for another four years by the Hornby family, so that would present them no immediate problems, but it seems to have been made clear that the family wished to sell the Raikes Hall and its land once this lease extension had expired. The cost to purchase Raikes Hall was impossible for them in terms of cost. It was around this time that Mother Cornelia, the founder of the Convent School, decided that more permanent accommodations were required and something that was owned outright by the school instead of being under the dictates of a leasehold property that didn't give them any long-term security. Decisions were quickly made, and always seemingly one step ahead, Mother Cornelia already had her eye on a suitable and affordable plot of land on which a new school could be built. Documents in the archive of the school have this entry for the period:

"The lease of Raikes Hall having nearly expired, negotiations were actively entered into for the purchase of land at Layton Hill & (sic) a bazaar to raise funds towards this was organized by Mother Gertrude Day, the energetic Superior. It met with great success. The school at this time numbered 50 pupils & (sic) was patronized by members of the Old (sic) Catholic families of Lancashire."

It would seem that the Sisters and the school had a good relationship within the local communities surrounding Raikes Hall. However, there were tragedies during their time there and these seem to have been exploited by suspicious locals towards anything or anyone associated with the Catholic Church. The Sisters faired no better as a result of this maliciousness and vitriolic gossip by some. It has to be remembered that there was still much suspicion and indeed prejudice exacted toward Catholics at this time. All an unfortunate consequence of the dissolution where even being a practicing Catholic in private was punishable by law – if not seen as treasonable and punishable by death! Certainly in the early years after dissolution. It seems extreme punishment, but there was such religious turmoil unleashed by King Henry VIII that it took centuries to heal the conflict caused between the Catholic Church of Rome and the newly created Church of England.

It is testament to the power of this gossip and rumour that still today some tell dark stories of what happened when the sisters were resident at Raikes Hall. Secret tunnels in the basement so they could sneak away in the night for carnal trysts with men from other Catholic orders. All nonsense of course as there were no other orders established in the area when the sisters were resident at Raikes. The existence of a Jesuit male order in the area didn't arrive until fifty years later when in the 1920s the St Joseph's College and School opened on Newton Drive.

It is testament to the strength of the rumours started nearly 150 years ago that they still exist in some form or another today. It also seems extraordinary that after such a short stay at Raikes Hall, the tenure of the Nuns created so many myths and legends – the subject of the tunnels was just the tip of the gossip iceberg!

The tunnels were, beyond doubt, actually built by Butcher to enable him to secret away his ill-gotten wrecking gains and also have the practical purpose of connecting the main hall with the stables and barns so that once dismounted after a long ride he and his friends could access the house in stormy weather without suffering unduly. In 1755 it was recorded in Blackpool records that:

"The Fylde Coast had its share of Shipwrecks…[the cargos would be spirited away] before the Coast Guards or Excise Officers could get to the wreck."

No doubt some of this cargo was spirited away through the tunnels at Raikes Hall for safe storage in the cellars without being seen by any officials who may have been keeping watch on the Raikes Hall. The tunnels would have been equally useful for spiriting stolen goods out of the house without being seen so they could be loaded up in the stables and ridden away in case of an impending raid by the Excise Officers.

There is an interesting story regarding Fox Hall that is worth retelling as Butcher was friendly with the Tyldsley family who owned that Hall and used to ride there with them onto the sands – in the latter part of the 18th Century, there would have been little in the way of buildings between the two estates. Tyldsley was a monarchist during the civil war and it has been noted that:

"[at] Fox Hall he entertained the Gentry of the district [including Butcher] including horse racing on the Hawes.

There is no evidence to suggest that he was involved with Butcher and Wrecking, but his fortunes dwindled and he ended up selling Fox Hall. Eventually it was turned into a public house – one still exists to this day on the site with the same name of Foxhall.

On a lighter note, and one the Sisters themselves would have perhaps smiled at, instead of being horrified by, was the recorded wreck of 1755 "of the ship named 'Travers' [which] was wrecked on the [Fylde] coast, it had a huge cargo of Lace, and there was [subsequently] 'Travers Lace' in homes all over the Fylde for years after!" Another wrecked ship was carrying among other delicacies a large cargo of dried peas and became known locally as "The Pea Soup Wreck" on account of its contribution to household meals.

There was also tragic deaths at Raikes Hall when some of the girls were taken seriously ill and died. This was not as a result of cruelty or mistreatment, as the gossips delighted in saying, it was sadly because of an outbreak of Cholera at the school. It would seem that illness and death brought fear to communities, especially when they did not understand why these terrible illnesses happened. Someone had to be blamed and it seems that as Catholics the school and the Sisters were an easy target for frightened locals. Cholera, we now know, is spread through the water supply when it is contaminated by waste or sewerage. Anyone drinking the contaminated water is in danger of contracting the illness and is in real danger of dying as a result.

Another rumour had one of the Sisters at Raikes Hall giving birth to a baby as a result of a clandestine tryst with a man. She then proceeded to drown the child in a pond in the grounds. This is of course nonsense and again it was gossips exaggerating the sad facts as reported in the Preston Guardian on Saturday, June 12th, 1869, after an inquest had been held there. The headline shouted thus:

"DEAD BODY OF A CHILD FOUND IN A POND NEAR A CONVENT AT BLACKPOOL"

The report went on to details the story in a less sensational way than the headline indicated.

"On Sunday evening last, as some of the inmates at the convent of The Sisters of the Holy Child were out walking in the grounds adjoining the Convent house, on Raikes-Hill, Blackpool, they discovered what seemed to be a bundle, floating in a pond.

Having got it out, it was found to be the body of an infant. The police authorities were communicated with, and on Tuesday an inquest was held on a body, at the police-station, Blackpool, before M. Myers. Esq., coroner, and after the evidence had been given, the jury returned a verdict that 'The child found in the pond was stillborn.'"

It seems pretty conclusive that there were no ulterior motives on the part of the Sisters; or that any of them or the pupils were involved in the tragic abandonment of the stillborn child. Had they been, then it is unlikely they would have informed authorities and brought attention to themselves, the Convent or any of their charges. Perhaps local gossips had heard that Mother Cornelia Connolly had been married [she made no secret of her past life], had children before becoming a nun, and that two of her infants had died? It is not hard to see how this kind of information can be misconstrued by local gossips – with much glee no doubt – and twisted beyond recognition.

History tells us that there have been many occasions when a desperate woman has left her newborn child, usually illegitimate, on the doorstep of a convent or church. It would seem in this case that as the child had been stillborn, it was abandoned in a place where it was thought nobody would find it. The greater tragedy in this story is the initial lack of dignity for the infant – that however was put right with a more suitable burial once the autopsy and inquest was complete.

Mother Cornelia was rightly proud of the school she had nurtured and visited often. She had sought out and found the Raikes Hall and deemed it suitable for her ambitions. She had also instigated the search for land where they could build their own Convent School, and found a plot of land at Layton Hill. She made things happen. Her spirit lives on today in the new school that now occupies Layton Hill Convent – St Mary's Catholic Academy.

"Through the years of growth and change, [Mother] Cornelia had not been forgotten. The love she had for the foundation, which she visited more than 20 times, was reciprocated and her spirit cherished. Not surprisingly many vocations to the Society came from Blackpool. One of the best-known photographs of [Mother] Cornelia was taken at Raikes Hall next to the desk which had been carved there. The Convent Annals tells us that 'a very nice Holy Child Spirit had grown with the school' and that in June 1870 Cornelia came to pay her last visit to the school [at Raikes Hall]."

Mother Cornelia also made sure that all the fruit trees and roses they had planted at Raikes Hall were moved to the new Gardens at Layton Hill. She also contributed to the design layout for the new school. It would be her lasting legacy.

For the Raikes Hall and its grounds the time had come when it would be reborn anew as a place of pleasure and entertainment. The irony is that the Sisters had moved there from Queen Square near the promenade to escape the noise, temptations and bustle of such frivolities. As they moved on, the same frivolities would flourish as a group of entrepreneurs saw their chance and seized it. The Raikes Hall and its lands would soon grow and develop into the Royal Palace Gardens.

Chapter 3

VICTORIAN PLEASURE OPPORTUNITIES

The scarcity of available Blackpool sea front land during the 1870s caused potential developers to look further inland. Despite the Raikes Hall's more easterly aspect, it's economical potential was obvious to a group of local entrepreneurs. Luckily, to their delight, the prestigious Raikes Hall Estate came on the open market and they made their move. A local cabinet maker, business man, and ambitious visionary, Joseph Smith, along with jeweller Adolph Moritz Viener, headed a syndicate that raised the £14,000 asking price.

Joseph Smith was a more than enthusiastic disciple of innovation, completely attuned with the Victorians' desire to be amused and entertained. Smith had traveled extensively in search of entertainment ideas. He and Viener were also shareholders in the North Pier and the Claremont Park development. Their combined business acumen was the ideal foundation for the development of the site. The syndicate also included: Ebeneezer Fowler (Draper), Jonathan Read (Sea Water Baths), J. Leonard, Henry Fisher, W. Birch, James Howard, and the local Gazette founder John Crime. Included in the sale agreement was the Raikes Hotel and its adjacent 33 acres, the Didsbury Hotel on Whitegate Lane (now the No. 3 Public House) – Whitegate Lane became Whitegate Drive years later as the area slowly gentrified as Blackpool expanded – and a row of desirable cottages at the Church end of Park Road, together with two pews and an interest in the running of St. John's Church.

So it was that circa. 1870 a new company was formed – Raikes Hall Park, Gardens and Aquarium Company – with a working capital of £25,000 (twenty five thousand pounds). A not inconsiderable sum for the time.

Shareholders invested £5 (five pounds) per share for the privilege of a dividend in the said company.

Almost immediately the new company engaged Ralph Rushton and John Fish as the respective secretary and manager. The engagement of Fish was to pay dividends during the company's formative years. Fish was well known on the northern recreational scene, most of his knowledge being attained through his connection with Manchester's famous Pomona Gardens.

During 1871, the Raike's enthusiastic directors, along with Fish, cunningly came up with a competition open to anyone in the land. It's purpose to afford a practical design for the Raikes Hall Gardens. Three cash incentives were offered for the winning entries. First prize £70 (seventy pounds), second £30 (thirty pounds), and third £20 (twenty pounds). The first prize was awarded to a Mr.Thomas Lewis Banks, a local south shore designer, and taking second prize was 32 year old Thomas Parkinson Worthington. Needless to say the local gossips generated an interest in the development of the new Pleasure Gardens and the possible entertainments to be available within. All of which created a buzz of publicity in the wider press and by word of mouth – the kind of free advertising eclipsing any that could be paid for.

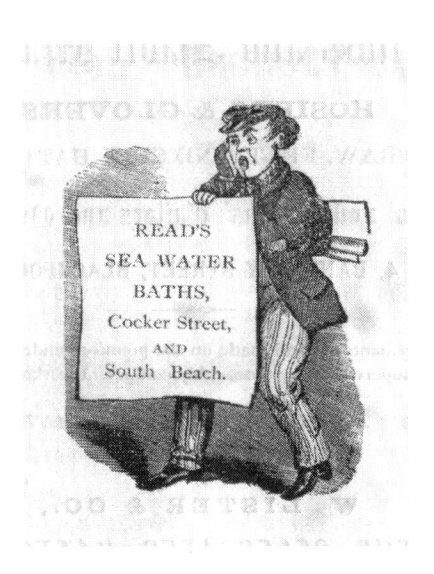

Read's Baths – Reads Avenue was named after the family. Popular baths during the 19th Century and into the 2oth. Their popularity about to have competition with Raikes Hall's development. Indeed Jonathan Read was part of the Gardens business syndicate and had a financial interest.

Bank's winning plan was imaginative and included: Vast formal lawns with intricate inlaid rose and flower beds. Continental style walkways and shaded paths. A huge 50,000 square foot dancing platform. A large well furnished indoor lounge and a large comfortable hotel. Also included in his overall plan were large open spaces where football and cricket could be played and the jewel in his winning plan was a large tropical conservatory, the most colourful and ornate outside of London. The plans, although ambitious and complex were adopted by the directors as they wanted something that would truly stand out and draw in the vast crowds needed to run such an enterprise and make it financially viable for the shareholders. They would interweave all the latest technology and fashions of the time and create conservatories for tropical plants and ferns that would emulate the famous Crystal Palace – thus ensuring the grounds could attract visitors in the winter months too. Visitors were drawn from all parts of the country and not just the north west.

The development of these ambitious plans from drawing board to reality was undertaken by many of the north's leading tradesmen and artists. Vast hordes of carpenters, stone masons and landscape gardeners descended on the project. Local master joiner Jacob Parkinson and Revoe Brickmakers, James Cardwell & Brothers, played major roles in the construction of the site. Throughout 1871 the Raikes became a hive of activity and the urgency of the work, came to a final conclusion, when the partially completed grounds were open to the public on Whit Monday 1872. Sadly, despite all the hard work by so many, and as many good intentions, the public's initial response was rather luke-warm. Some of the more ambitious structures were not finished in time for the opening, so many were quite rightly disappointed. The company quickly responded, in an effort to save some face, by dropping the entrance fee to 3d (three pennies) for the rest of that holiday week. It worked and they managed to keep the attraction open as other work went on in the background. Once the season was over, work could start again in earnest. It was in many ways a false start and the management would have been better advised to delay the opening until the following year. However, it did generate some welcome, and much needed income, to help cover the cost of completing unfinished projects in the grounds.

As a result of these difficulties in the first year, even more improvements were made to the grounds and their facilities for the following year of 1873. It was also decided that a line up of top London and international variety acts were the key to keeping the public happy and ensuring financial stability. The summer season show was born. It has to be remembered that the Gardens had to compete with other Blackpool attractions, the North

Pier and new South Pier [now Central Pier]. To allow a financial comparison to be made and to put this into context, during Whit week of 1873 North Pier attracted 61,250 paying customers and its rival South Pier had slightly less at 59,500 but this was increased by a further 18,200 passengers on steamship excursions to and from Conwy and Llandudno that operated from the North Pier daily. The revamped Raikes Hall Gardens admitted nearly 40,000 paying customers over the same four day period that year.

These figures give a fascinating insight into the popularity of Blackpool, and the sheer number of visitors arriving by packed trains in the resort, and how the structured holiday weeks [Northern wakes weeks and Glasgow and Edinburgh fortnights] would dominate the core trade to the town in the decades to come. The wakes are described thus:

"The wakes week is a holiday period in parts of England and Scotland. Originally a religious celebration or feast, the tradition of the wakes week developed into a secular holiday, particularly in the north west of England during the industrial revolution [in 19th century]. In Scotland each city has a 'trades fortnight' or two weeks in the summer when tradesmen take their holidays.

Grand Avenue & Drive.

This view looks towards the Aviary with the Ballroom and Indian Village to the right. Continuing round the bend would bring you to the Raikes Hall Hotel. Looking down after entering the main gates towards Whitegate Drive. The lake and sports ground would have been to the right.

Although a strong tradition during the 19th and 20th centuries, the observance of the holidays has almost disappeared in recent times due to the decline of the manufacturing industries in the United Kingdom and the standardization of school holidays."

The wakes were at their height during the development of the Rakes estate and the Gardens opening to the public. At that time most people took daily train excursions from their town to Blackpool; in later years the affordability of the guest house allowed the same working class people to spend a few days in the resort. Droylsden poet, Elijah Riding (1802-1872), sums up the wakes week in his popular poem 'The Village Festival'

"There is a merry, happy time,
To grace withal this simple rhyme:
There is jovial, joyous hour,
Of mirth and jollity in store:
The Wakes! The Wakes!
The jocund wakes!
My wandering memory now forsakes
The present busy scene of things,
Erratic upon Fancy's wings,
For olden times, with garlands crown'd
And rush-carts green on many a mound.
In hamlets bearing a great name,
The first in astronomic fame."

During Oldham wakes week circa. 1860, according to John Walton's book Leisure in Britain, over "23,000 holidaymakers traveled on special trains to the resort during wakes week from that town alone." Strange as it seems to us today, the whole town would have their holiday together in the same week – meaning that everything closed down and everyone took their day excursions at the same time. This meant that communities literally lived, worked and had their day trips and holidays together in the same place! No getting away from work colleagues or neighbours as all the faces on the promenade or in the Raikes Gardens would be familiar ones.

The popularity of the Gardens during 1873 was beyond question, thousands continued to stream through the turnstiles. A general entrance fee of 2d (tuppence) had been eventually decided on and was the right balance between economic success or failure. On many occasions, given the right weather, the open air dancing platform, overlooking the ornate and colourful Italian Gardens, attracted an average of a thousand couples per day. For those feeling less energetic, morning and afternoon promenade concerts were more than popular on the vast Raikes Hall terrace.

Encouraged by a forthright directorship, many local Blackpool and Fylde agricultural societies used the vast open spaces of the grounds. The Raike's monopoly of the Blackpool holiday trade was reflected in an application to the local Brewster licensing sessions. Almost in touching distance from the Raike's boundary wall stood the Belle Vue Strawberry Gardens. Owner, John Hodgson, when applying for a spirit license during September 1873, outlined to the authorities his financial investment in the Belle Vue (what remains of the Belle Vue still exists today and is a public house on Whitegate Drive under the same name). Hodgson had spent several thousands of pounds, or so he claimed, developing the grounds of the Belle Vue. This resulted in over 700 customers a day passing through his turnstiles, and during peak season over 6,000 customers had been known to frequent the hotel grounds. Hodgson who had lived in the Belle Vue for many years, remarked to the licensing authorities that his establishment and Gardens may not be as aristocratic as the Raikes and its Gardens but was still visited by respectable people; and thus worthy of a liquor license as well. Indeed the Raikes Gardens did monopolise the local holiday trade. This was borne out by the management of the No. 3 Hotel with a similar opinion as that overlooked the Raikes and Gardens (still a public house bearing the same name today on Whitegate Drive). There was some sour grapes that the success of the Raikes and its Garden attractions was dominating trade in the area – this is all too often the case when one business tends to outgrow others in its vicinity and they suffer as a result.

Royal Palace Gardens entrance at Church Street & Park Road junction. The Salvation Army Citadel (the old Grammar School) now occuupies this site. Circa. 1874

However, one local man welcomed the holiday crowds to the area. Thomas Mycock, proprietor of the resort's Royal Hotel, on the promenade, who lived near to the Gardens. He also owned a large tract of land bordering the eastern side of the Raike's estate. The area on Whitegate Lane between the No.3 and the Belle Vue was known locally as 'Mycocks Field'. It was here that amateur athletics meetings were held, but its main claim to fame was for Blackpool Horse Races to take place on this land. This area now has a row of imposing accrington brick Victorian Villas, built in 1893 overlooking the Royal Palace Gardens, on its Whitegate Drive edge of the fields.

During these formative years the Raikes played an important role in the promotion of goodwill in the community. Many local people, in particular the old and very poor, benefited from fetes and other such parties organized as a result of the benevolence of the Raike's directors. It was obvious during the early 1870s that the Raikes and its neighbouring licensed premises comprised an area of entertainments and recreational developments arguably without equal in Blackpool's colourful history.

Raikes Hall's Gardens attracted a wide range of clientele from merchant bankers to paupers. This in turn promoted, without intention, it could be argued, a seamier side to the surrounding area. Ladies of the night plied their trade and pimps, pickpockets and conman abounded – although in a minority. All attracted by the potential for lucrative pickings. These undesirables, and the innocence of many others, created an atmosphere charged with energy and excitement, the whole reflecting the kaleidoscope of life at the time.

Early development of the Gardens – the Conservatory with Raikes Hall to the right clearly visible with landscaping in the foreground.. Circa. 1874

By 1879 the Gardens were firmly established and were a source of great pride to the management and to the local economy that benefited from the success. The official leaflet for the Gardens was published to afford publicity for the forthcoming season. This was written by a journalist at the time know as Mr. Nemo, and was reproduced in the press far and wide. His style is formal, descriptive and delicious in the way it brings to life the famous Gardens. He draws you into that lost world and one can imagine his voice and his enthusiastic delivery:

"Raikes Hall Gardens are so well known to the thousands who annually visit our shores, from the different parts of Lancashire and Yorkshire, that it almost seems unnecessary to expatiate, at any length, on the many attractive features which are so familiar to visitors and residents alike. For some years now these famous Gardens, partly owing to the beautiful manner in which they are laid out, but, probably, more owing to the exertions and enterprising spirit of the Company's indefatigable manager, Mr. John Fish, have enjoyed an amount of popularity which has never waned, notwithstanding that, during the last two seasons, places of amusement in Blackpool have been considerably increased, and people have, to a certain extent, been spoiled with having so many establishments to select from when pleasure seeking. As each season comes round, however, the old familiar crowds are to be seen flocking to Raikes Hall; the grounds daily thronged with thousands of people; the Pavilion is filled at each representation of the spectacular piece and, at night, when fireworks commence, the coloured lights show up a sea of faces that is not easily to be forgotten. Frequently as I have described the Gardens it is always a source of pleasure to me to enter on a new tour of investigation; and often as I have wandered through the extensive grounds, and familiar as I am with every nook and corner, yet I always discover some fresh beauty, and return to my study like 'a giant refreshed.' Having recently, through the courtesy of Mr. Fish, the manager, and Mr. Shuter, the head Gardener, renewed my acquaintance with scenes that are daily growing more beautiful, and having obtained information that will be of interest to my readers, I propose to describe, as graphically as I can, the whole establishment, and to give the fullest details possible, on the grand entertainments provided for the season of 1879.

"And, first of all, THE GROUNDS, which cover an area of nearly 40 acres, and are most tastefully laid out in walks, shrubberies, bowers, ornamental beds, borders, drives, &c., deserve a passing notice. The wide carriage drive and walks have been put into thorough order for the season, and the flower beds and borders leading from the entrance gates to the Hotel present not only a tidy and trim appearance, but are bright and gay with colour from a combination of beautiful plants newly bedded out. Throughout the grounds the foliage is to be seen in spring beauty, and the shrubberies are looking their best, the early showers and the genial sunshine having brought out the tender leaves in that lovely green which is only to be seen in the early summer. The lawns are as smooth as velvet, and he must be a clodhopper indeed who has to be requested to 'keep off the grass.' The shady bowers are suggestive of lovers' whisperings, and wherever the eye rests the Gardens are 'with verdure clad,' and a delight to all lovers of nature.

"For an agreeable promenade, I know of nothing to surpass THE TERRACE, and, if Mr. Fish will only restore the seats, I can conceive of nothing pleasanter than resting here awhile and gazing on the landscape below, and beyond it. There is a wealth of foliage in perspective, whilst immediately beneath the Terrace are artistically laid out beds, which are planted with bright hued flowers and which are really gorgeous with colour. As something like 100,000 plants in bloom are to be seen in different parts of the grounds, and the bulk of these have been bedded out underneath the watchful eye of Mr. Shuter.

Raikes secondary carriage entrance at the junction of Hornby Road & Park Road – with gate-house. The advertisement on the left of the gate is for the reenactment of the Battle of Balaclava. The gardens were renowned for these realistic battle entertainments.

Ferneries, Skating Rink & Conservatory.

The Gardens were quickly renowned for their botanical excellence and the tropical ferneries were hugely popular in the Victorian period. Walkways and carriage drives made the gardens a tranquil experience by day and night.. Circa 1880s

"THE GRAND CONSERVATORY AND SKATING RINK are particularly worthy of attention, the former being one of the finest in England, and the latter one of the best of its kind. It is always summer in the Conservatory, and even in the depth of winter, when the keen wind whistles through the leafless trees, and the grounds are utterly devoid of interest, bright flowers greet the eye, and the perfumed air makes 'glorious summer' of the 'winter of our discontent.' To wander round the continuous promenade of 200 years, which constitutes this floral hall, is no ordinary treat, and for a visitor to Blackpool to return home without having feasted his eyes on the thousands of plants to be found in this delightful department, is to miss one of the grandest sights to be seen in the neighbourhood. Mr. Shuter, the talented head Gardener, never seems to be weary of rearranging the Conservatory, and in anticipation of the season has made alterations and additions which have resulted in a tout ensemble which is perfectly dazzling and bewildering in effect. The exhibition this year is a horticultural show, which could scarcely be surpassed, for exquisite taste in arrangement, perfection of growth, and the rare specimens everywhere conspicuous. Some of the plants are not only costly, but are rarely to be met with in England. The Skating Rink occupies the centre of the building; it has a large and smooth area for skating upon; the Plimpton skates are kept in excellent condition; and courteous attendants are at hand to supply everything required by rinkers. A first-class band performs here, daily, popular selections. There is a bar at which refreshments of good quality are dispensed at reasonable charges, a most convenient smoke-room, lavatories, &c.

"The Raikes Hall show of plants is not by any means confined to the grand Conservatory, as at the top part of the grounds there are numerous GREENHOUSES, VINERIES, &c., which will well repay a visit, and, in fact, ought not to be missed. Since last year a great improvement has been affected by pulling down the partition walls in several of the chief range plant houses, which shows off plants to far greater advantage, and enables visitors to obtain a better view of the specimens. Of these five central houses it is difficult to say which is the most attractive, as each contains such a variety of plants in full bloom that at every turn some new beauty of form or colour meets the eye, and the climax is never reached. The Show House contains some magnificent specimens of Dracaee, Bourgainvilla Glabra, Hibiscus rosea sinensis, Eucharis Amanzonica, Lomaria Gibba, Palms, Crotens, a profusion of beautiful maidenhair Ferns, and an almost endless variety of showy plants.

Ball Room, Indian Village & Dancing Platform.

This image shows the Raikes Hall [far right on the line of buildings] with the Indian Pavilion and Village and the Ballroom building attached. In front of this huge area was also an open air dancing platform that was very popular with the Victorian pleasure seekers. In the foregorund you can see the steps leading down to the Italian Rose Garden and the famous Fairy Fountain – the fountain had jets that sprayed up to 100 feet in the air. This view would be seen from Whitegate Drive (between Bryan Road and Forest Gate) looking towards town. Circa. 1890s

The Rose House is in splendid condition, and is a great attraction to the lovers of this lovely flower, the beautiful tea roses growing in great profusion, together with those named 'Marshal Neil,' 'Adam,' 'Duc de Magenta,' 'Catherine Merinet,' 'Madame Darnaizin,' 'Sounvenir de Paul,' 'Neron,' and others, all of rich growth, and which are to be seen in great perfection. Another department, under the same roof, contains a fine show of camelia plants, and in addition to some large and handsome trees in full bloom, the roof is literally covered with Stephonitis, Depladinia Brierleyana, &c., which have a facinating influence, for it is difficult to tear oneself from the spot. To leisurely walk through these five (glass) houses, as they are to be seen at present, and to gaze on the exquisite tints of some of the flowers, the various shades of green in leaf and ground, added to the perfumed air, is most refreshing to the eye and to he brain. I have never seen this particular branch of Mr. Shuter's field of labour when it was presented so charming an appearance, and can readily understand the fostering care and watchfulness that is requisite to bring such an extensive collection of plants to such perfection. Near the show and propagating houses are the VINERIES, Pelargonium House, Cucumber House, and an extensive area devoted to frames n which plants are hardened previous to being bedded out; roses are grown, and a variety of plants reared. To pass a eulogium on Mr. Shuter's ability as a high class Gardener is quite unnecessary, as his various departments speak louder and more gracefully in his praise than I could. Suffice it to say, that whatever part of the Gardens you visit, you see traces of great care and a result of practical knowledge, combined with a thorough love of botany in all its branches.

"The Great Pavilion occupies the most prominent position in the grounds, it is 154 feet in length, 72 feet wide, and 48 feet high. It has an unusually large stage, two spacious galleries, and will accommodate an audience of 5000 persons. The Ball Room, adjoining the mammoth dancing stage, is another fine building, and is used for dancing, there being also here provided cloak rooms, parcel offices and lavatories. The Dancing Stage is probably the largest in the provinces, has a spring floor, seats all round, an elegantly designed orchestra for the band, and is brilliantly lighted at night. There is a spacious and well kept bowling green near the ball room, a cricket ground, a racecourse, used at agricultural meetings and athletic sports, and a large lake well supplied with pleasure boats. The hotel and restaurants are all excellently fitted up, and dinners, teas, and refreshments of the best quality may be had at most reasonable charges. A large number of servants are employed in connection with the different departments, and all of whom will be found to be courteous and attentive to the requirements of visitors. Having hurriedly glanced at the principal erections in the grounds I must now give fullest particulars concerning the entertainments provided for the season."

Mr.Nemo brings it all vividly to life and helps us today to understand the enormous scale and complexitiy of the Gardens. The Raikes Hall at its centre served as an Hotel and also offered bars and restaurant facilities – at that time attached to the Grand Pavilion and its enormous indoor theatre and entertainment space. Today the Raikes is a public house and seems somewhat forlorn considering its past glory at the very centre of Blackpool's ultimate Victorian attraction.

The Gardens were well and truly established and the delights of the horticultural attractions and its oppulent facilities were only surpassed by the artistes and entertainers who performed there during the long seasons. As we shall discover, it attracted the very best and most famous of those artistes.

This view of the Grand Opera House, Gardens and fountain. As you entered the Gardens at Church Street, you would pass the boating lake and the sports field as you proceeded towards the theatre. Raikes Hall, the Indian Pavilion and Ballroom, Bars and Billaird Rooms lay on the other side of this building. Circa. 1880s

[COPYRIGHT.]

GUIDE

TO THE

Raikes Hall Gardens

BLACKPOOL

Reprinted, by special permission, from Nemo's Journal.

PRICE ONE PENNY.

Printed by Lomax & Son, Cookson-street, Blackpool.

Mr. Nemo's Guide to the Gardens, Circa. 1880

This view of the Gardens shows the Opera House and the sports field (left) with the boating lake situated to the right.. Circa. 1880s

A post card view of the Gardens – that clearly shows the sports field, grandstand (left) and the boating lake to the right. This would have been before the Grand Opera House was added to the many attractions of the Gardens.

The Graphic – An Illustrated Weekly Newspaper – kept pleasure seeking Victorians with up to date news and advertisements for the Royal Palace Gardens.

Chapter 4

MUSIC HALL & VARIETY ARTISTES EXTRAORDINAIRE!

In 1873 Adolph Viener chaired the Raikes Hall Companies annual general meeting. On the agenda was the announcement that, due to ill health, one of the Raikes founding fathers, Joseph Smith, intended to retire from the board.

On the economic front, accounts proved that some 248,000 visitors had passed through the Gardens turnstiles which produced profits of £2,445 1s & 9d. This was boosted by a further sum of £12,222 0s & 1d from the sale of lands surplus to requirements. With this foundation of financial prosperity, the Gardens directors embarked on a vast spending programme.

Early in 1874, the impressive new entrance gates were constructed in the finest Portland stone. They would grace the North West corner of the estate at the top of Church Street. Grand in scale and classical in design the gates had two large central archways for those who arrived by private horse and carriage, and two pedestrian entrances at either side. Built each side of these palatial gates were the lodge houses where the gatekeepers and their families resided to assist when the Gardens were open to visitors and for security when the Gardens were closed. Three other entrances on Raikes Street (now Church Street), the far end of Hornby Road near the junction with Park Road, and another on Whitegate Lane (now Whitegate Drive) opposite Forest Gate junction were added. These three additional gates also had small lodge houses and a single carriage central arch with two pedestrian arches either side. During the same year the new gates were constructed one of the countries leading horticulturalists, a Mr. Burrows, was engaged to oversee the complete refurbishment of the tropical conservatory, principally the introduction and siting of some 100,000 native and tropical blooms and plants.

The large ornamental lake first cut and escalated in 1872 was, by 1875. Filled to the brim and had bedded into the landscape. The trees and plants had matured enough to give it a natural look. During the summer months the lake was a hive of activity, pleasure boats gave enormous fun, watched delightedly by hundreds of picnickers sitting upon their rugs on its grassy shores. Some thirteen bars supplied or fortified their food and drink needs. Beer and porter was drunk in enormous quantities.

Nearby, the Belle Vue Strawberry Garden proprietor, Hodgson, was alarmed at the growth of the Gardens. However it was not all bad news for his business, the Raikes Gardens undoubted success during the 1870s had a knock on effect on the fortunes of its rivals.

In about 1877 the Gardens were at the height of their popularity. Cultural marvel was added to the entertainments with the construction of a large, Victorian gothic style, Grand Opera House. Skating was also very fashionable and the directors decided to release funds for the construction of a 300 yard, round roller skating rink. However, skating did not come cheap, patrons had to pay 6d for the pleasure, although this included the hire of the Plimpton's skates.

With the increase in visitor numbers to the Gardens and its increasing popularity it started to impact on the local area – simply because of the vast numbers of people visiting both the Gardens at the Raikes but also the No.3 Hotel and the Belle Vue Strawberry Gardens. The worst congestion was at the junction of Whitegate Lane by the Didsbury Hotel. Letters flooded into the local Blackpool newspapers confirming the dangers. One letter stated that it was fortunate nobody had been killed, considering the devil may care attitude of the many cabbies taking the Church Street corner in such a reckless manner.

Monkey House & Aviary

The Monkey House and Aviary were very popular with the Victorians. All situated in splendid, manicured gardens that created fine vistas and walkways. Inside the heated conservatories the visitors could marvel at exotic birds and creatures from far-off lands they had only seen pictures of in books. Circa. 1880s

The social fabric and respectability of the Whitegate Lane area was also a concern. Locals were unhappy by the increasing number of prostitutes and their entourage of minders and pimps. Some houses were presenting a facade of respectability, but we're in fact nothing less than dens of iniquity!

For a period the economic benefits of visitors being attracted to the area worked well for the Belle Vue Strawberry Gardens. Entertainment there was also in full swing and famous music hall acts graced the stage – along with its speciality of fresh strawberries and cream - along with refreshments that were of the alcoholic variety! The huge ballroom, completely rebuilt after a fire some years earlier was booming. The late night drinking patrons were happy to take advantage of the fact the premises was divided by a local boundary line for licensing purposes. This meant the bar in the Marton side had to close a half an hour earlier than the bar on the opposite Blackpool side of the ballroom. The patrons happily crossed the ballroom to the later bar when the time came each evening!

Suddenly in 1887 Blackpool auctioneers James Butcher offered for the sale the ongoing concern that was the Hodgson's Belle Vue Strawberry Gardens. It was debatable why the Whitegate Lane hostelry came onto the open market – it seemed to be doing well but the reality was it was struggling to be financially viable as the attractions in the neighbouring Royal Palace Gardens were added to and improved. Also a factor was Hodgson's ongoing altercations with the licensing authorities. As it turned out the public auction was also a flop. After an initial bid of £16,000 the bids went up by £250 stages reaching a limit of just £20,000 before being withdrawn by Hodgson.

Meanwhile the Belle Vue's other neighbour, and rival to the Royal Palace Gardens, the Didsbury Hotel was also becoming more popular. It's fine grounds, good ale and music hall entertainers pulled in the crowds by the hundreds. In May of 1878, proprietor Sarah Hawks opened, at considerable expense, a purpose built theatre. All these efforts were to enable them to compete with their famous neighbour that now bore a Royal title in its name.

The Royal Palace Gardens at Raikes Hall seemed unstopable and impossible to compete with on any kind of level playing field for its smaller neighbours. The sheer variety and scale of the entertainments on offer, along with spectacular firework displays, is almost impossible to explain in a way that would do them all justice. Suffice to say that the Victorian's did not do things by half measures. Indeed, it would be impossible to replicate because the costs incurred would be prohibitive today. Mr. Nemo, from Nemo's Journal, again describes for us the attractions on offer within the Gardens during the 1879 season:

"Taking the musical part of the programme first, three splendid bands of picked musicians have been engaged for the summer. One will play for skating to in the Rink, another will constitute the Pavilion Orchestra, under the direction of talented pianist and conductor, Mr. Saville Swallow, whilst a band of 26 performers, including several fine soloists, and conducted by Mr. Walter Chapman, will play for dancing from one o'clock each day on the great stage. This band has been styled, not inappropriately, that of the Raikes Hall Guards, for new and magnificent scarlet and gold uniforms and brass helmets and plumes, in exact initiation of those worn by Her Majesty's Life Guards, have been specially provided, and will give the band a very imposing and attractive appearance.

For the outside show, so popular last year, the celebrated [French] Silbon Troupe (five in number) have been engaged. Their performance is positively marvellous, and some of their feats are such as 'no other artistes in the universe can accomplish.' Their tricks include some very daring gymnastic feats in mid-air, a terrific flight through space by the boy 'Eagle', who turns a double summersault and catches the hands of Monsiour Silbon at a height of 40 feet. A female member of the troupe also accomplishes a number of difficult feats at great altitude.

In the Great Pavilion will be produced, throughout the season, every afternoon and evening, Mr. John Fish's grand spectacular representation of 'the Afghan War, or the storming of Ali Musjid.' The whole of the scenery has been specially painted for this production – which has been some months in preparation – by the eminent firm of Messrs. T. Grieve and Son, of London. The Afghan dresses have been designed by Mr. W. T. Gauntlett, of London, and the British uniforms have been manufactured on the premises by Mr. W. G. Chapman. The uniforms are an exact counterpart of those worn by the British and Afghan troops, the guns, swords, and accoutrements generally are equal to those supplied to the army, and the stage accessories are in keeping with the perfection that characterises the entire production."

The battle reenactments were so popular at this time as they conveyed in a visual format the very battles that the British Army were actually fighting and making history with across the world. There were no televisions or cinema screens and no radio at this time to give accurate accounts – only the newspapers carried the stories and not everybody was able to read or could afford to purchase regular newspapers. But, more of this later when Mr. Nemo actually describes one of these reenactments that was staged at the Gardens to thousands of spectators nightly.

Undoubtedly many of the visitors to the Gardens were lovers of the sensational, as such they were attracted by one of the acknowledged masters of the high wire, the original 'son of the desert', the 'African Blondin'. This great artists act was unique within a select rank of high wire performers. All of his contemporaries used the hollow of their feet to clasp the rope, whereas Blondin used the heel and toe method. Included in his breathtaking performance was the extraordinary feat of Blondin carrying a heavy cooling stove to the centre of the rope – forty feet off the ground – watched by a breathless, silent multitude below. On reaching the centre, he astonished them by kindling the stove, lighting it, and cooking an omelet in front of their very eyes, all the while balancing on his high wire. Thousands of fans throughout the world, including crowned heads of Europe, had witnessed his bizarre antics. He drew them to the Gardens in their thousands and he never disappointed. Accompanied by their roars of approval he would twist, spin and summersault off the high rope to the ground to take his bows.

In complete contrast to the high wire drama of Blondin was the firework displays created by the 'King of Pyrotechnics' himself, Robert T. Bruce. The Manchester based Bruce designed and implemented bespoke firework displays to order. His Raikes presentations were topical and spectacular. Many of his productions were a recreation of some recent military campaign. In one such production nearly one hundred local school children were engaged as extras. They were dressed in military regalia and marched and counter-marched with precision in front of realistically painted scenic backdrops. This, and the effect of the fireworks, made the reenactments more than convincing to the vast crowds watching.

On a more genteel note, the Raikes ornate ballroom proved irresistible to the Northern dancing fraternity. They danced with gusto to the popular polka, mazurka, quadrilles, and the lancers! Strict tempo was provided by a convincing, yet pseudo, military band ornamentally attired in blue uniforms resplendently finished with yellow cuffs and insignia.

During the long lazy days, innovation was the name of the game and the Gardens played their part. The medieval pastime of hawking was introduced to enthralled visitors. Mr. Barry's famous flying hawks were engaged following a successful tour of the European capitals. The hawking performances had their fair share of incidents. On several occasions the trained Hawks took flight from the Raikes grounds in pursuit of some seagull or pigeon. Mr. Barr spent some considerable time retrieving his charges as far afield as Poulton and Staining!

Royal Palace Gardens

RAIKES HALL GARDENS COMPANY LIMITED

GRAND EXHIBITION OF PLANTS AND FLOWERS
IN THE LARGE
CONSERVATORY
AREA 31,000 FT

THE ORIGINAL AFRICAN

BLONDIN

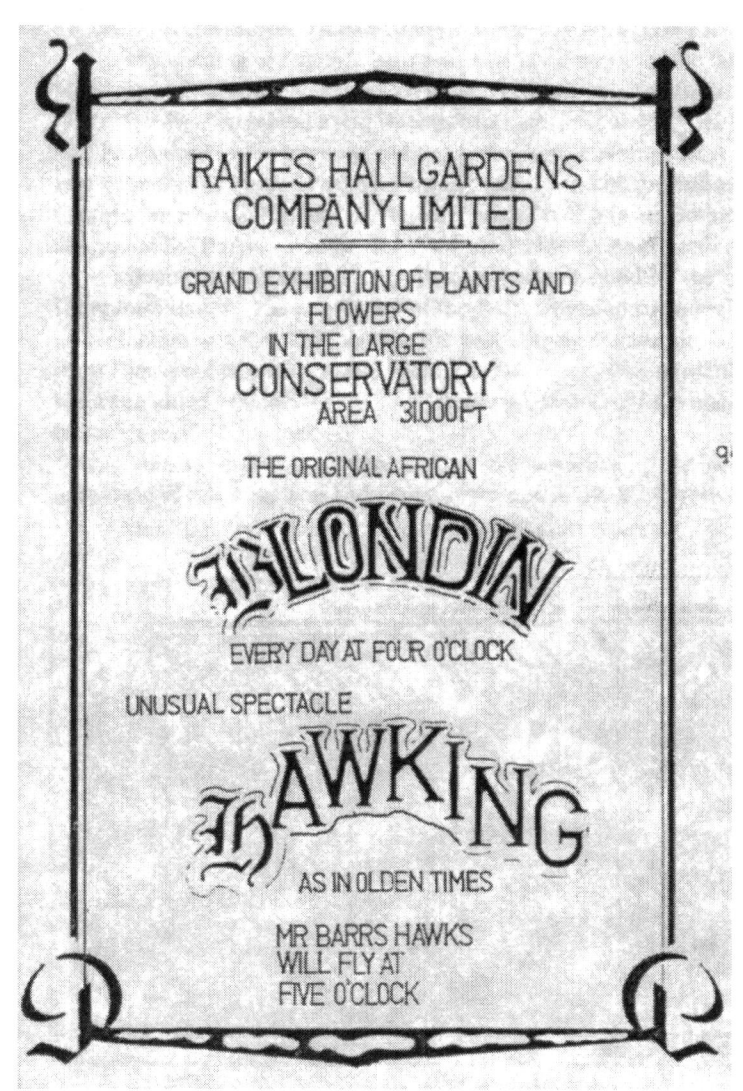

EVERY DAY AT FOUR O'CLOCK

UNUSUAL SPECTACLE

HAWKING

AS IN OLDEN TIMES

MR BARRS HAWKS
WILL FLY AT
FIVE O'CLOCK

The Advert for the African Blondin's appearances at the Gardens

Mr.Nemo of Nemo's Journal explained in detail the wonderfull reenactment of the Afghan War that was played out nightly at the Gardens. On reading his account one can only wish to be somehow transported back to that time and witness the show first hand. It is little wonder that visitors came away thrilled and delighted at what they had seen played out before their very eyes:

"Through the courtesy of Mr. Fish, I am enabled to give an outline of the entertainment and a synopsis of the scenery and incidents. The panorama opens with an exceedingly picturesque view of the city of Cabul, showing the bazaar or market place, with the gate in the background. The picture is full colour, contains plenty of figures, and will bear looking at longer than there is time for, as the Ameer with his staff officers and attendants at once come upon the scene. A message is brought my the British mission seeking admission to the Khyber Pass, which Shere Ali immediately refuses, calls up his army, and makes preparations to repulse the British troops. The Afghan army is then reviewed and put through a number of evolutions, and marches off into the country to meet the English and Indian forces. The panorama then moves on from Cabul to Candahar. In the extreme distance are the mountain ranges, with a view of the city of Candahar, whilst in the foreground are groups of Afghans with their camels resting. Then comes the town of Thrull, on the other side of the Khyber Pass. This is a fine mountainous view, with the town in the middle distance, the foreground being occupied with brushwood and cannons lying about suggestive of a scrimmage having recently taken place.

"Scene 4 is a magnificent view of the rugged heights of the Khyber Pass. The huge rocks tower up in awful grandeur, whilst the half-hidden ravines are frightful to behold, being partially obscured by overhanging portions of the mountains. Here the first meet the contending armies takes place, when there is some cross firing which ends in the retreat of the Afghans. The next scene is a sort of jungle, showing the country through the Khyber Pass, and represents an elephant battery advancing to the front. The British troops here halt for the night, pitch their tents, and enjoy themselves with sports. The Highlanders go through a number of Scottish sports and games, a number of elephants are put through a performance, and then camp fires are lighted and the troops retire for a night's rest before resuming their march; the scene being flooded with moonlight, and the effect being very picturesque. They are soon roused up, however, by the arrival of an aide-de-camp from Sir Samuel Brown; preparations are made to receive the general; there is the mustering of the armies; the General arrives and reviews the troops, putting them through a series of manoeuvres, soldiers are called to the front from the surrounding country, until the stage is completely filled,

Royal Palace Gardens

THE KHYBER PASS:

SCENE FROM THE
AFGHAN WAR
AT RAIKES HALL.

Image of the famous scenic display for this entertainment. From Nemo's Journal Guide Book. Circa. 1879

and then the whole army is marched off in order. This scene is one of the most effective in the whole piece.

"The panorama then moves entirely away, and reveals the great set scene of the Fort of Ali Musjid, which is a magnificent picture. Here will take place the meeting of the British and Afghan troops, the grand attack by the former, under the command of General Sir Samuel Browne, the repulse of the latter, victory for the English, on the heights of the now famous Fort, the planting of the British standard and tableaux. The magnificent series of pictures which Messrs. Grieve and Son have placed on the stage are a triumph of the serene painters art. I should mention that, previous to each representation of war, the Borthers Spence, who are described as 'the gens of the burlesque profession,' will give a laughable entertainment consisting of character delineations of the most eccentric kind.

"The round of entertainments will wind up as in past seasons, with a grand display of fireworks, by Mr. Bruce, and which will consist of many novelties, and the Falls of Niagara in liquid fire, on a greater scale than has hitherto been attempted. Mr. John Fish, the energetic and courteous manager, has exerted himself to the utmost to place before his patrons a series of entertainments which, for variety and general excellence, could scarcely be beaten, and the whole of which can be enjoyed for sixpence, and extra charge only being made to the reserved seats in the Pavilion, and a small charge of admission to the Grand Conservatory. Whilst Mr. Fish continues to issue annually such a liberal programme, and the Gardens are kept in such splendid condition, there can be little doubt that, despite the counter attractions in the town, Raikes Hall's Royal Palace Gardens will be pronounced by visitors and others to be 'the place to spend a happy day.'"

Opposite is the La Belle Rose Spiral. She would walk on a ball to the top and then walk it back down backwards! She retired to Blackpool and lived on Mere Road until her death in 1947. (see Biography in reference section)

Royal Palace Gardens

Raikes Hall, Opera House, Grand Conservatory and Lake.

La Belle Rose Spiral

COUNTY AND LANE ENDS HOTEL.

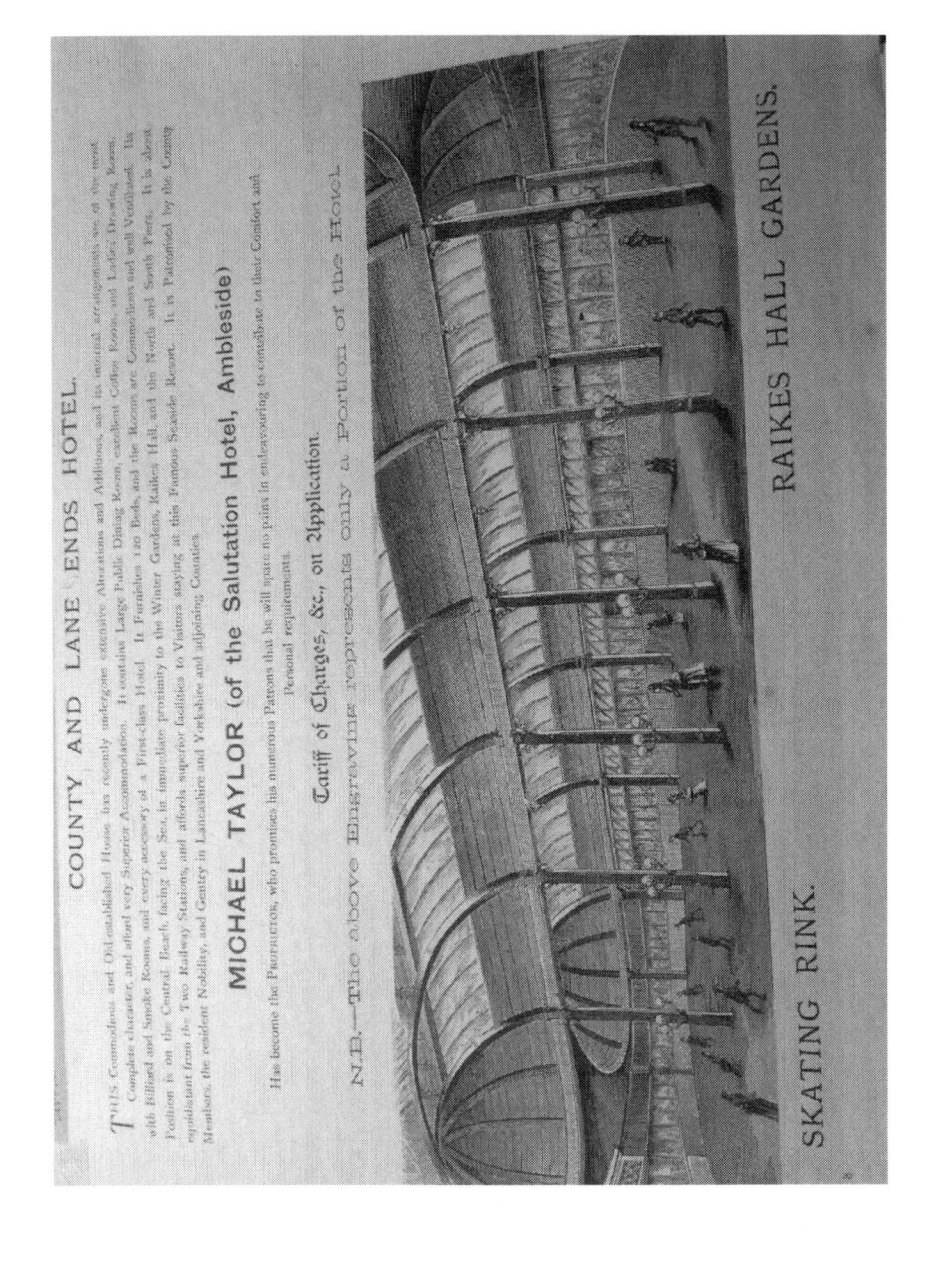

THIS Commodious and Old established House has recently undergone extensive Alterations and Additions, and its internal arrangements are of the most Complete character, and afford very Superior Accommodation. It contains Large Public Dining Room, excellent Coffee Room, and Ladies' Drawing Room, with Billiard and Smoke Rooms, and every accessory of a First-class Hotel. It Furnishes 120 Beds, and the Rooms are Commodious and well Ventilated. Its Position is on the Central Beach, facing the Sea, in immediate proximity to the Winter Gardens, Raikes Hall, and the North and South Piers. It is about equidistant from the Two Railway Stations, and affords superior facilities to Visitors staying at this Famous Seaside Resort. It is Patronised by the Leading Members, the resident Nobility, and Gentry in Lancashire and Yorkshire and adjoining Counties.

MICHAEL TAYLOR (of the Salutation Hotel, Ambleside)

Has become the Proprietor, who promises his numerous Patrons that he will spare no pains in endeavouring to contribute to their Comfort and Personal requirements.

Tariff of Charges, &c., on Application.

N.B.—The above Engraving represents only a Portion of the Hotel.

SKATING RINK.

RAIKES HALL GARDENS.

Royal Palace Gardens

General Manager, W. MORGAN.

Raikes Hall Gardens.

GORGEOUS DISPLAYS OF

FIREWORKS

AT DUSK DURING THE SUMMER.
"THE FALLS OF NIAGARA," in Liquid Fire.

REFRESHMENTS OF THE BEST QUALITY.

Special Notice.—July 10th, 1880.

MYERS' GREAT AMERICAN HIPPODROME & CIRCUS.

The Largest Company in the World, from Paris, Crystal Palace, Royal Agricultural Hall, and Alexandra Palace. 200 HORSES, PONIES, ELEPHANTS, LIONS, CAMELS, &c. Roman Races, Chariot Races, Steeplechases, Pony Races. COOPER IN THE DEN OF LIONS. The Performing Elephants. The Tug of War—One Elephant pulling against 50 Men. The Elephant Swimming in the Lake.

The Performances will take place each Afternoon in the Open-air HIPPODROME, and each Evening in the NEW MONSTRE CIRCUS.

PLANTS, &c., from 6d. to 20 gs. each, on Sale or Hire.

WEDDING BOUQUETS, WREATHS, &c.,
ON SALE.
APPLY TO THE HEAD GARDENER.

Special Arrangements made with Excursion Committees for Admission or for Dining, &c.

SEE OTHER ADVERTISEMENTS.

PLEASE NOTE.—There is more covered Accommodation at these Gardens than at all other Places of Amusement in Blackpool put together. Visitors can drive into the Grounds and alight at the Pavilion, Rink, Circus, Hotel, &c., without suffering any inconvenience from the weather.

History of Raikes Hall

WAR IN CHINA — TO-NIGHT!
GO AND SEE THE GIGANTIC
OPEN-AIR FIREWORK PICTURE
EVERY NIGHT

REPRESENTING THE
CITY of CANTON
DESIGNED AND PAINTED AT TOWN HALL
Representing the Great Battle between the British & Chinese.
Entire destruction of the Chinese Fleet.   Canton in Ruins!
This Thrilling Spectacle will be produced EVERY NIGHT

The Royal Palace gardens held nightly spectacular firework displays as a finale to the days events and entertainments. The open air Dancing Platform was also used at night in the summer – weather permitting!

Looking towards the Aviary and Monkey House (left) and the Ballroom and Indian Pavilion & Village (centre). The boy is looking towards Whitegate Drive – this is the main drive after entering the main gates to the Gardens.

Chapter 5

COMPETING ATTRACTIONS

Change was coming. Another important addition to the future of Blackpool as an entertainment Mecca was the opening in July 1878 of the £100,000 architectural masterpiece that was Thomas Mitchell's Winter Gardens. The directors of the Royal Palace Gardens could see the economic threat that the new Winter Gardens represented yet they were generous in their reception of the VIP's and guests attending the opening functions – ironically held at the Royal Palace Gardens! As part of those events they also arranged a fantastic firework extravaganza in the Gardens to celebrate the opening of the Winter Gardens. Firework wizard Robert Bruce enthralled the gathering dignitaries with his Falls of Niagara! Every type of firework and pyrotechnic released their colourful effects. Rockets by the thousand, comets and dragons, and immense star bursts illuminated Blackpool's skyline.

Supplementing the firework displays was the Thomas Grieve and Sons outdoor diorama, 'The Crescent and the Cross'. Dioramas, actually large outdoor paintings, were the fashion of the era, and the Royal Palace Gardens featured Grieve's masterpiece to thrill the crowds. What a wonderful sight it was for the promenaders, and those in their carriages, to behold his 6,000 ft. canvas of paint and colour depicting recent events in the Turkish-Russian War. Night and day-time scenes of Constantinople, Adrionople by moonlight, and the road to Plevna, all painted with clarity and realism. To add to the effect, local military drill instructor Charles Exley organized and trained over 100 local school children to portray the opposing armies – marching to a mock battle. One can only imagine the thrill of this spectacle for a public who had no other form of entertainment to bring current events to life. Newspapers could report the conflicts and news from far away places and have a few black and white photographs, but that was all. Most people never went abroad or travelled far beyond where they were born, so these kind of visual entertainments and paintings gave the events life and colour and most importantly, drama!

There was a strong sense of community responsibility and benevolence on the part of the directors of the Gardens; and it has to be said many other of the businessmen in the surrounding area. During the 1870s and 1880s it was an area where the Royal Palace Gardens excelled. Workhouse kids and the town's old people benefited from their generosity. Knife and fork teas were provided for hundreds with servings of roast beef, corned beef, boiled ham, tongue and brawn. It may seem average fair to us, but to the poor of the late 19th Century it was a luxurious treat and food they could not have afforded to eat on a daily basis, if at all in some cases.

The famous Niagara Cafe buildings. The circular building had a huge cyclorama depicting Niagara Falls painted by the famous French artist Phillipatoux. The building in front was the cafe for visitors after they had viewed the exhibit. Circa. 1880s

Artist Phillipatoux working on one of his scenic masterpieces for the Gardens famous battle reenactments. He also painted the famous Niagra cyclorama.

The other entertainments on offer, at these charity events and most other times of the year, were an exciting selection. The Roller Skating Rink was very popular amongst old and young alike, with scientific roller dancers Gosling & Wright the stars in that arena. In the large Indian Village Pavilion musical entertainment and dancing was provided by the Saville Swallow Orchestra. Those with less energetic aspirations could marvel at the huge painted cyclorama in the Niagara Cafe – giving them the thrill of experiencing what it would be like to see the actual Niagara Falls. The real thing being half way across the world meant for ordinary folk it was highly unlikely they ever would see the falls in any other way. However, to add excitement the Gardens again contracted the famous high wire performer Blondin to replicate his famous high wire crossing of the falls in the Royal

Palace Gardens – they had a special high wire erected for him near to the Niagara Cafe for the purpose. It was thrilling and the next best thing.

On the sporting front, Rugby football appeared at the Royal Palace Gardens in 1879. It was played on the already popular football pitch located by the grandstand and racing track. One of the first encounters was Chorley v Rossendale. Chorley came out tops with one try and three touch downs to Rossendale's one.

On the face of it the 1879 Season, from the public's point of view, was as popular as ever. However, behind the scenes, a change of personnel was thought necessary, mainly to increase the marketing and popularity, not to mention the finances, of the Gardens. As a result the company appointed an energetic and charismatic Thomas Grundy as the new manager of the Royal Palace Gardens and all its attractions and amenities.

Encouraged to be bold and adventurous in his booking of attractions, Thomas Grundy followed their instructions. Through the pages of the national and local newspapers he embarked on an advertising campaign aimed specifically, but not exclusively, at the industrial workers of the Northern towns. One of the first bookings to come from this campaign was a block booking for some 400 employees from the works of T.W. Mitchell from Wakefield. The Yorkshire visitors were entertained by the popular 35th Lancashire Artillery Band, ably supported by the in-house Band of the Raikes Hall Guards. Local favourite Leotard Bosco was the master of ceremonies and throughout the summer of 1880 he was the mainstay of the season.

In spite of the success of these advertising schemes the directors, and the Garden's management, were always open to new ideas and potential attractions. They reacted to public interest in and demand for the experience of balloon flight – then a hot topic in the newspapers of the time. As a result the celebrated aeronaut Captain J.A. Whelan from Huddersfield was booked to appear with his balloon in May. Captain Whelan was the countries leading exponent on the art of balloon flight and his appearance at the Gardens, in spite of some weather problems was a big hit and drew massive crowds to witness the marvel of flight – even though most experienced by watching the Captain from the ground! Still, it was beyond thrilling for the visitors of the time and equally so to speak to and listen to the Captain's stories of daring do!

These excitements, and the dancing that followed in the ballroom or the open dancing platform weather permitting, were finished off with spectacular firework displays. Additional transport was laid on between the Gardens and Talbot Road's North Station for the many who wanted to witness the balloon flights and nightly fireworks. In addition to the Ballooning, another popular attraction performing at the Gardens that season was Rastus the Flying Man. And fly he did, but not in a balloon! His act involved him undertaking death-defying stunts on high ropes which

culminated in a grand final that would see him plummet to the ground to the horror of those watching. At the last moment, instead of being splattered on the ground, he would be elevated again at speed via the rope attached to his ankles – surely the precursor to bungee jumping. Those watching were thrilled, amazed, horrified then gasping with relief all within a few seconds. Unforgettable entertainment that would chatter and gossip its way into thousands of ears – all of whom would make their way to the Gardens to witness it for themselves.

On the same bill that season was another French artist, Monsiour Albin, billed as 'The Iron Horse Champion Of The World'. His unique act involved his acrobatic performance on a monster cycle with its 18ft 9inch driving wheel. If that wasn't enough sensationalism for the 1880 season, the spectators hadn't reckoned on Herr Holtum. John Holtum was the 'King Of The Cannon' which title may give a clue to his act. Indeed he commanded one of the highest fees in the history of the Gardens attractions. His act included catching a 9lb cannon ball fired from his cannon. Tricks with cannon balls weighing 20lb, 32lb and 64lb (think unbelievable juggling!). Firing a 300lb field shot loaded with powder and cannon ball – the explosion and the noise horrendous and terrifying in equal measure. In the early stages of developing the act, he was advised not to attempt to catch a cannon ball fired at him. He ignored the advice, but had two fingers blown off his left and as a result. He recovered and mastered the technique – his lost digits didn't seem to impede his unique ability. He would also challenge any gentlemen to try and pull a rope out of his clenched teeth – his strength described as being like that of 2 to 4 horses. One can only wonder at the skill of this man and how he managed to have the strength and tenacity to pull off his various thrilling tricks.

The early 1880s would see the arrival at the Gardens of one of the world's most famous travelling circus'. After several attempts it was finally agreed and deal was struck with the renowned Myers American Circus. Accommodating the travelling circus did not come cheap. The management initially spent nearly £2,000 to build a monster indoor arena. Under the expert supervision of Mr. Langley, ably assisted by foreman Mr. Rough, the structure represented the largest purpose built circus in Europe.

Royal Palace Gardens

Balloonist Captain Whelan – the 'people's William'

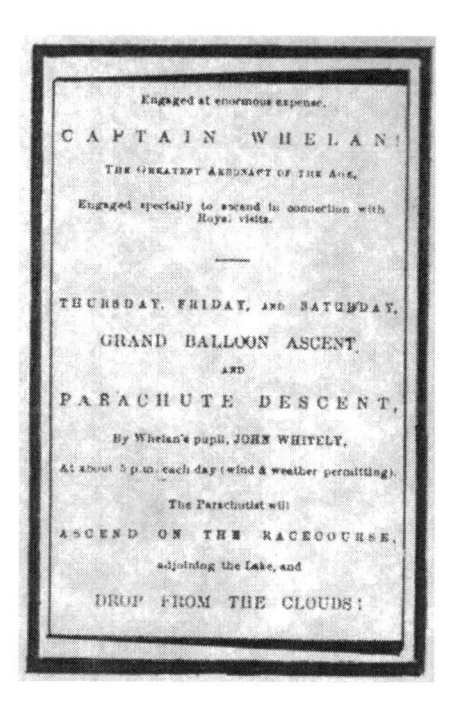

The main building housed the impressive centre ring that was 45ft in diameter which was illuminated by a fantastic array of gas jets comprising of of 14 pendant chandeliers lit by over 200 mantles.

Myer's Circus was famous for its animal acts – most especially their horses. Stables sited at the south side of the ring housed over twenty horses and forty ponies. At the opposite end of the building was a tiles and well drained stables capable of holding another 42 horses. Adjacent to the main circus building was a specially constructed amphitheatre almost 85 yards in length with a width of 65 yards, where over 5,000 spectators could be seated at each performance. Admission to the grounds was 6d, then a further payment was charged for entrance to the Hippodrome and Circus. 2 shillings (first class seats), 1shilling (second class seats), 6d for the gallery. The standing promenade area was free but sightlines for the show were limited.

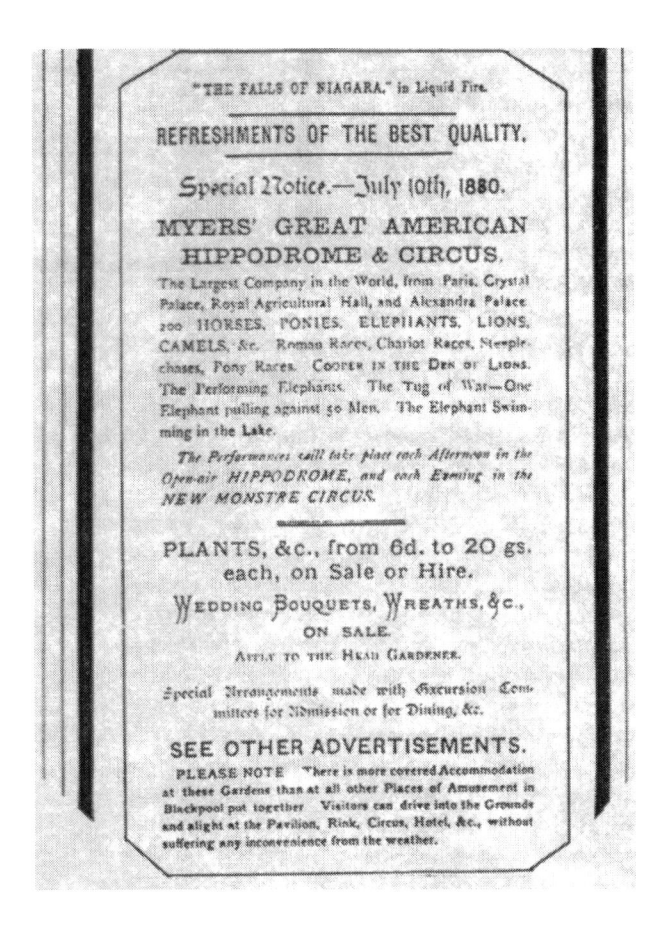

> "THE FALLS OF NIAGARA." in Liquid Fire.
>
> REFRESHMENTS OF THE BEST QUALITY.
>
> Special Notice.—July 10th, 1880.
>
> MYERS' GREAT AMERICAN HIPPODROME & CIRCUS.
>
> The Largest Company in the World, from Paris, Crystal Palace, Royal Agricultural Hall, and Alexandra Palace. 200 HORSES, PONIES, ELEPHANTS, LIONS, CAMELS, &c. Roman Races, Chariot Races, Steeplechases, Pony Races. COOPER IN THE DEN OF LIONS. The Performing Elephants. The Tug of War—One Elephant pulling against 50 Men. The Elephant Swimming in the Lake.
>
> *The Performances will take place each Afternoon in the Open-air HIPPODROME, and each Evening in the NEW MONSTRE CIRCUS.*
>
> PLANTS, &c., from 6d. to 20 gs. each, on Sale or Hire.
>
> WEDDING BOUQUETS, WREATHS, &c., ON SALE.
>
> APPLY TO THE HEAD GARDENER.
>
> Special Arrangements made with Excursion Committees for Admission or for Dining, &c.
>
> SEE OTHER ADVERTISEMENTS.
>
> PLEASE NOTE "There is more covered Accommodation at these Gardens than at all other Places of Amusement in Blackpool put together Visitors can drive into the Grounds and alight at the Pavilion, Rink, Circus, Hotel, &c., without suffering any inconvenience from the weather.

Myer's Circus capitalized on their international reputation – in Europe they were the favourite of many Royal Houses. It's star performers included Rose Myer and her celebrated troupe of show horses. Little Valdo the famous clown and his brother Tom Felix; English champion jockey Tom Watson and his acrobatic skills on horseback; Alivanti the King of the Loose Wire; and the world famous Trackene Horses, purchased directly from the King of Prussia; Sagrino and his magnificent equestrian exploits, with musical accompaniment provided under the baton of the celebrated musician and conductor, Herr Schultz.

The shows finale always had a heightened element of drama to thrill the crowds. A giant Elephant lumbered into the arena carrying a metal structure that was a telescopic cage. It was then assembled with the help of the Elephant and several stage hands to form a large caged enclosure. Then, through a cage tunnel a number of ferocious lions entered the arena - and were joined in the said cage by famous Lion Tamer extraordinaire, John Cooper. The local Blackpool Gazette newspaper reviewed his performance:

"Mr. Cooper goes in amongst the ferocious creatures, his caresses and endearments and honeyed words to the powerful beasts and the spectacular effect can never be forgotten when once witnessed!"

When weather permitted, the open air arena became the Garden's focal point – a centre of equestrian excellence. Roman Chariot racing, horse and pony racing, linked with unparalleled feats of horsemanship – adding to the thrill and majesty, not to mention strength, of six performing elephants.

Raikes Hall Gardens.

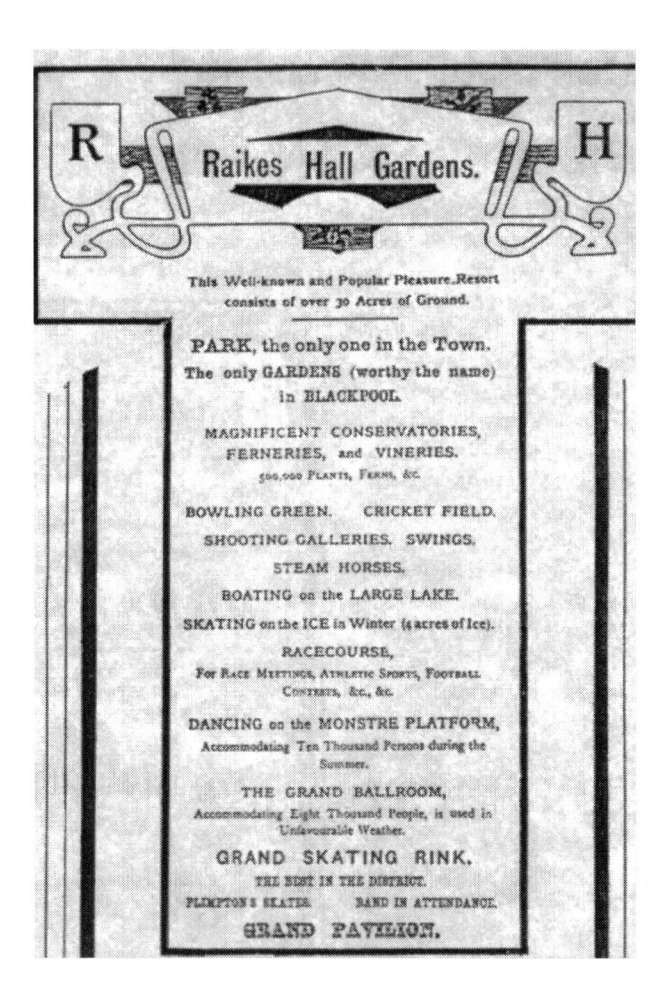

This Well-known and Popular Pleasure Resort consists of over 30 Acres of Ground.

PARK, the only one in the Town.
The only GARDENS (worthy the name) in BLACKPOOL.

MAGNIFICENT CONSERVATORIES, FERNERIES, and VINERIES.
500,000 Plants, Ferns, &c.

BOWLING GREEN. CRICKET FIELD.
SHOOTING GALLERIES. SWINGS.
STEAM HORSES.
BOATING on the LARGE LAKE.
SKATING on the ICE in Winter (4 acres of Ice).
RACECOURSE,
For Race Meetings, Athletic Sports, Football Contests, &c., &c.

DANCING on the MONSTRE PLATFORM,
Accommodating Ten Thousand Persons during the Summer.

THE GRAND BALLROOM,
Accommodating Eight Thousand People, is used in Unfavourable Weather.

GRAND SKATING RINK,
THE BEST IN THE DISTRICT.
PLIMPTON'S SKATES. BAND IN ATTENDANCE.

GRAND PAVILION.

This advert pre-dates the renaming to the Royal Palace Gardens in 1887. The choice of activities is impressive – also the numbers catered for, "accommodation for ten thousand" on the outdoor Dancing Platform. This was probably exaggerated just a little! The Victorians liked to do things in a big way.

Chapter 6

TROUBLED TIMES
THE SHOW MUST GO ON!

The period throughout the late 1870s and early 1880s were arguably the Garden's golden years. Thousands of people took a stroll or a carriage ride through the grounds for the entrance fee of 6d. The Garden's easily accessible on foot from North Train Station. The same could not be said for the Garden's near neighbour the Belle Vue, that venue having more than its fair share of problems.

Belle Vue proprietor, John Hodgson, was fighting a long drawn out argument with the local council. Blackpool Corporation improvement schemes included the laying of new sewer and drainage facilities along Whitegate Lane (now Whitegate Drive). Hodgson blamed the disruption caused on the dramatic loss of trade because access was restricted quite severely. It would seem he was justified in his complaint, but the council seemed to disagree and did little to compensate him. His fresh strawberry and cream trade took a big hit. Where he would normally sell some 10,000 quarts of strawberries at 8d a quart, in addition charging 2d for a glass of milk, and 6d for fresh cream and sugar (enough for six plates of strawberries), the drainage works caused him to lose nearly two thirds of his business with the result being near ruin.

The truth was that visitors tastes were changing and they preferred the spectacular events in the Royal Palace Gardens, the attractions offered at the Winter Gardens or the North Pier and the promenade. Little did they realise that this contraction of the entertainment areas would also claim the Royal Place Gardens in time. However in 1881 the optimism was still high and the Gardens still popular – especially the announcement of a new circus attraction for the following season.

As a direct result of the successful 1880 circus season, the following year another famous circus was booked. Charles Hengler's Circus specialised in equestrian entertainment, and his specialty was the famous representation of the infamous Highwayman Dick Turpin and his ride to York. It realistically featured the Royal Mail coach and four horses, Turpin's attempt to hold up the coach and rob its occupants. It had pathos aplenty when, as a breathtaking finale, Turpin's faithful horse, Black Bess, came to an untimely end. It was a death scene worthy of any stage, and the horse was trained to perfectly reenact the death scene – aided by Hengler himself who played Dick Turpin to perfection and elicited roars of approval from the huge spell-bound audiences.

All seemed well, but behind the dramas there were other dramas going on in the shape of continued financial struggles for the Gardens. Radical changes were decided and quickly implemented by the board of directors. It came in the form of George Bart Taylor, who was promoted to a senior management position. Taylor was renowned for his passion, energy and enthusiasm for the best entertainments, so the board instructed him to bring his magic to the Gardens and make them the centre of entertainment excellence. To aid his development of the Gardens they placed a large sum of money at his disposal. He quickly set to work and one of his first actions was to engage John Holmes Glover as his assistant manager and overseer of the entertainments in the Gardens.

One of the first artistes to be engaged was Frank Gilfort, a famous high wire performer who demanded an enormous fee to appear. Worth every penny for the crowds he would bring to the Gardens – all paying an entrance fee and spending in the Gardens refreshment areas. Glover also had great plans for the theatre and the Indian Pavilion – the perfect venues for his extravagant theatrical ideas. With his bosses approval, Glover also engaged the Sisters Zagaro, described as wonderful lady acrobats, joined by the incomparable Miss Bertie Stokes, the duettists and dancers The Latuo Sisters and Miss Maggie Hunt from the infamous Oxford Music Hall, London. Zoro, the wonderfull equibrilist, joined the line up for the 1881 season along with the final headliners the famous White Minstrels.

Jonathan Reads untimely death in 1892 surprised the Gardens directors. He was only 42 years old. The Read family had played a leading role in the economic fortunes of Blackpool. They had originated from the hamlet of Worsthorne near Burnley, and Jonathan's father, William, had elevated the family from simple beginnings. He originally sold hawker pots (pots and pans from a cart going from street to street with his wares) and as a result he prospered enough to build the Reads Market and then the popular Sea Water Baths on the promenade. Eventually William encouraged his son Jonathan to invest in the town's developing entertainment scene – it was this foresight that made him invest in the original syndicate that purchased the Raikes Hall complex and Gardens to create the famous attraction. Jonathan's death was a blow and many of those he worked with were truly grief-stricken that he should die at such a young age and at a time when he had such ambitious plans for the Gardens to take them into the future.

RAIKES HALL GARDENS
RIFLE RANGE
AND SCHOOL OF MUSKETRY
A CONTEST
WILL TAKE PLACE WED AND THURS
26TH. 27TH SEPT. 1883.
ENTRANCE FEE 1 SHILLING
PRIZES
1ST A NEW REMINGTON RIFLE.
2ND A LARGE HANDSOME DOUBLE ELECTRO PLATED CUP.
3RD NEW SIX CHAMBER REVOLVER
ENTRANCE FEE WILL PAY FOR SHOTS

Today the Health & Safety officials may have something to say about this – especially as they sometimes used live ammunition!

The board decided that they would go ahead with Jonathan's vision for the Gardens and agreed to spend a large amount of money redeveloping and adding to the Gardens attractions. The already popular Indian Pavilion went through many internal and structural changes that transformed it into an enormous and handsome theatre. The existing balcony was widened and strengthened and a marvellous new seating area was constructed opposite the main stage for three hundred and fifty people. The stage itself was added to and its thrust increased by nearly twenty feet, whilst backstage additions to the fly and scenery facilities to enhance the productions and give them more spectacle. Messrs Firth & Son (Manchester & London) we're responsible for the ornate decoration of the proscenium arch and the Pavilion interiors. A local painter from Abingdon Street, Mr. Turner, carried out other decorating contracts within the Pavilion and his impressive portraits of Shakespeare, Burns, Byron, Moorem, Motzart and Handel were much admired.

For the 1883 reopening of the Indian Pavilion a grand and spectacular presentation was devised – Aladdin and his Wonderful Lamp – under the direction of Lloyd Clarence. Other attractions that year included the Blackpool Volunteer Band for dancing and the sensational performance in the open air of the Fernandez Trio, a group of gymnasts. In the ballroom Professor Codman performed his Punch & Judy show.

The Gardens also presented in 1883 reenactments of famous battles that were most popular in national newspapers. That year it was 'Bombardment of Alexandria' a Firth &Son masterpiece. For this reenactment a colossal picture was prepared depicting the scene of the bombardment, with the forts, British Ironclads (naval ships) and Alexandria in the background. The technical detail was based on Messrs. Danson's famous achievements at the Belle Vue Gardens, Manchester. The structure occupied the space below the grand terrace at the eastern end of the Gardens. It was 150 feet in length and 40 feet high, and some 60 feet from back to front. Two of the ships were moveable and were manned by crews of actors – mostly local youths who enthusiastically volunteered their services. At each side of the picture was a tower, and in the centre of which stood figures of those who took a prominent part in the Egyptian campaign. The leading men were sculpted in fireworks, and the bombardment concluded with the grand pyrotechnic display. The total cost of the production was over £1,000. A colossal sum of money for the time.

A number of dramatic companies appeared throughout the 1883 season. They included Robertson and Bruce's Guvnor Company, Cruickshank and Collingwood's Redemption Company, Charles Bernard's and Bikee Taylor's Comic Opera Company, and Hubert Ogrady's Eviction, Gommach and Emigration Companies. In addition to this, throughout the season, Charles Allen's Circus was engaged and of course the marvelous tea rooms, dancing stage, skating rink, bowling green, swings and boats etc were all in full use. Also for the horse racing fans, the course constructed some years earlier was, following the completion of the 1883 racing season, to be widened and extended.

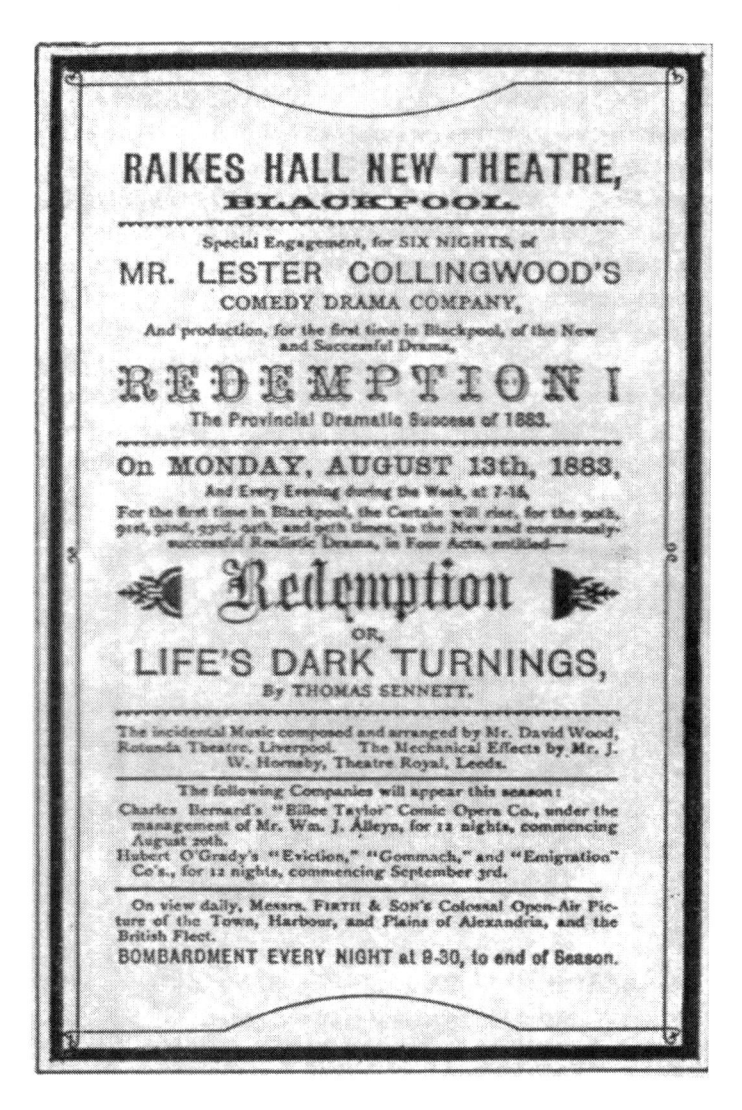

RAIKES HALL NEW THEATRE, BLACKPOOL.

Special Engagement, for SIX NIGHTS, of

MR. LESTER COLLINGWOOD'S COMEDY DRAMA COMPANY,

And production, for the first time in Blackpool, of the New and Successful Drama,

REDEMPTION !

The Provincial Dramatic Success of 1883.

On MONDAY, AUGUST 13th, 1883,

And Every Evening during the Week, at 7-15.

For the first time in Blackpool, the Curtain will rise, for the 92nd, 93rd, 94rd, 95th, and 96th times, to the New and enormously successful Realistic Drama, in Four Acts, entitled—

Redemption

OR,

LIFE'S DARK TURNINGS,

By THOMAS SENNETT.

The incidental Music composed and arranged by Mr. David Wood, Rotunda Theatre, Liverpool. The Mechanical Effects by Mr. J. W. Hornsby, Theatre Royal, Leeds.

The following Companies will appear this season:
Charles Bernard's "Billee Taylor" Comic Opera Co., under the management of Mr. Wm. J. Alleyn, for 12 nights, commencing August 20th.
Hubert O'Grady's "Eviction," "Gommoch," and "Emigration" Co's., for 12 nights, commencing September 3rd.

On view daily, Messrs. FIRTH & SON's Colossal Open-Air Picture of the Town, Harbour, and Plains of Alexandria, and the British Fleet.
BOMBARDMENT EVERY NIGHT at 9-30, to end of Season.

An impressive line-up of entertainment from 1883. Note the description of the outdoor cyclorama: "Colossal Open-Air Picture of the Town, Harbour, and Plains of Alexandria, and the British Fleet. During the reenactment of this battle a huge ship sank in view of the astounded audience at the

Gardens. All topped off with a fantastic firework display to end the drama! Not bad for 6d.

> "THE FALLS OF NIAGARA," in Liquid Fire.
>
> **REFRESHMENTS OF THE BEST QUALITY.**
>
> Special Notice.—July 10th, 1880.
>
> **MYERS' GREAT AMERICAN HIPPODROME & CIRCUS.**
>
> The Largest Company in the World, from Paris, Crystal Palace, Royal Agricultural Hall, and Alexandra Palace. 100 HORSES, PONIES, ELEPHANTS, LIONS, CAMELS, &c. Roman Races, Chariot Races, Steeplechases, Pony Races. COOPER IN THE DEN OF LIONS. The Performing Elephants. The Tug of War—One Elephant pulling against 50 Men. The Elephant Swimming in the Lake.
>
> *The Performances will take place each Afternoon in the Open-air HIPPODROME, and each Evening in the NEW MONSTRE CIRCUS.*
>
> PLANTS, &c., from 6d. to 20 gs. each, on Sale or Hire.
>
> WEDDING BOUQUETS, WREATHS, &c., ON SALE.
> Apply to the Head Gardener.
>
> Special Arrangements made with Excursion Committees for Admission or for Dining, &c.
>
> **SEE OTHER ADVERTISEMENTS.**
>
> PLEASE NOTE There is more covered Accommodation at these Gardens than at all other Places of Amusement in Blackpool put together. Visitors can drive into the Grounds and alight at the Pavilion, Rink, Circus, Hotel, &c., without suffering any inconvenience from the weather.

This advert from 1880 is also interesting for the sale of plants and flowers – the Gardens predated the Garden Centres we enjoy today. Also the last statement on this advert:
"Please Note – There is more covered Accommodation at these Gardens than at all other Places of Amusement in Blackpool put together. Visitors can drive into the grounds [horse & carriages] and alight at the Pavilion, Rink, Circus, Hotel, &c, without suffering any inconvenience from the weather."

TELLING THEM HOW TO USE THEIR SAFETY LAMPS.—The civic party—from left to right, the Town Clerk (Mr Trevor T Jones) the Mayor (Coun. Rhodes W Marshall, J.P.) and Ald. J R Quayle, J.P.—talking to Mr J L Smith, mine manager

She planned it 20 years ago

STAR OF THE 80's HAD WHITE FUNERAL

LA BELLE ROSE, pictured at the height of her fame (left) and a snapshot taken in later years.

"Alphonsine, La Belle Rose," one-time queen of the spiral, and one of the most spectacular figures in the variety of the 'eighties, planned her funeral 20 years ago to the last detail. On Wednesday she was buried at Blackpool Cemetery in the vault she then purchased.

SHE was buried, according to those long-ago instructions, in a white coffin dressed in the white silk she wore on the spiral, with her beloved jewelled chain, ivory cross and ear-rings.

The vault was lined with white chrysanthemums the entrance banked with them.

Few in Blackpool knew that Mrs. Augusta Caroline Rosalie Wingfield, who died in her 92nd year on Sunday, had one time been a beauty, a continental grande dame who used the best French perfume.

Her last appearance was at the Blackpool Hippodrome, when it was a variety theatre, just before the outbreak of the 1914 war. Since then she had lived quietly at her home in Merryroad.

ATTACKED BY WOLVES

Her father was Norwegian, her mother German.

She was born in Berlin, as a child travelled widely through Russia with her father's circus. Later near Moscow, when she was a star her sleigh was attacked on one occasion by wolves.

She became famous in Europe and Asia, topping the bill in Moscow, Kiev, the Moulin Rouge and the Folies Bergere in Paris. In America she was widely known.

In England she played at the Crystal Palace and the Alhambra in London, in Blackpool appeared at the Tower, Winter Gardens, and the now vanished Raikes Hall.

Her act was sensational. Standing on a ball, two feet in circumference, she manoeuvred it to the top of a 40 foot high spiral. Span of the spiral was 10 inches wide. She came down backwards.

LA BELLE ROSE in her sensational spiral act.

£200 A WEEK

She purchased the act from a man named Lizardo, who injured his spine in a fall, and who laughed at the idea of a woman attempting such a hazardous feat.

In Blackpool she was paid £200 a week, a big sum in those days. Her husband died many years ago.

When asked why she planned her funeral, she would say: "I have lived like a queen, I will die like one."

B.B.

La Belle Rose of the famous Spiral Act dies in Blackpool in 1947 aged 92

Chapter 7

BOTANICAL LEGACY & ROYAL TITLES

As we have heard from Mr. Nemo's Journal, a major attraction of the Royal Palace Gardens lay in its fantastic array of plants, shrubs, trees, verdant lawns and ornamental flower beds. With its piece de resistance resting in the splendours of the Grand Conservatory. It attracted the elite of the North of England's horticultural fraternity. Its charm portrayed by an abundance of semi-tropical plants, many collected from the far outposts of the Empire by the adventurous skills of the plant seekers. The plants displayed included: Cipredium, Barbatum, Clrendron, Blafouri, hundreds of Gardenias, Anthurium, Begonias, Glavinias, Stephonitus, Floribundas, Bougainvilla, and Indian Azaleas. The visitors entrance fee was augmented by the sale of all manner of plants ranging from botanical rarities to simple cut flowers at prices ranging from a few pence to an making £20! A precursor to the Garden Centres that would become so popular in the latter half of the 20th Century – so way ahead of its time in that respect.

Looking further at this enthusiasm the Victorians had for Gardens the Fylde coast had several to visit on a kind of grand botanical tour in the area. After the Royal Palace Gardens, and the nearby Belle Vue Strawberry Gardens, the next on the list was Marton's Cherry Tree Gardens. Open topped horse buses happily ferried people between the various Gardens for a small fee. During the 1880s the Cherry Tree Gardens were under the personal supervision of Mr. Ferguson, and even though they were a good ride from the Royal Palace Gardens, they had many admirers and those willing to visit. During the early days of spring was arguably the time to visit the Cherry Tree attractions, with the trees in full blossom, it's bedding plants laid out by the thousands, it's modest conservatory which housed a notable display of ferns and exotics, and the most famous of its attractions its Peach House.

On route was a stop off at the Oxford Pleasure Grounds where one could admire the Gardens, or relax with a game of bowls on the largest bowling green of its day. An abundant choice of liquid refreshment was provided including the delight of Dunvilles old Irish Whisky – served from wooden cask or bottle.

Another Garden on the tour was Carleton's Castle Gardens, the ideal place for a picnic and with regular carriage and wagon services available to and from Blackpool and the other Gardens. Captain Thomson's Castle Gardens played an important role in the Grand Botanical Tour. These may seem simple pleasures compared with the attractions and entertainments we have at our disposal today, but for the people of that time they were exciting and thrilling diversions from their daily working lives.

However, they were all side shows compared to the Royal Palace Gardens for size and opulence, but also for the grand palm houses and the ornate landscaped ground and attractions therein. It also boasted a Grand Terrace. Over 600 feet in length, it was, given the right weather, a focal point of glamour and splendour whereby the ladies of fashion and their suitably attired consorts paraded in style. During the day their purposeful steps were accompanied by the musical strains of a string ensemble or the velvety tones of a brass band. Many of the visitors to the Gardens, as was common in Victorian England, took a keen interest in the military campaigns of the British Army throughout the Empire and beyond – especially the battles where they fought and emerged victorious! Their patriotic interest was well catered for where many of the famous battles were reenacted on the vast open space just below the grand terrace. For those with an eye for competition the Gardens School of Musketry provided small bore rifle and pistol competitions throughout the season.

Arguably the 1886 season was the best prepared in the Gardens history. The more than enthusiastic manager, George Bart Taylor, planned it with precision. Taylor's organisational skills were second to none and had not gone unnoticed by many of Blackpool's entertainment entrepreneurs. The local Blackpool Gazette confirmed this through its pages thus:

"In Mr. G.B. Taylor the directors have at the head of their affairs a man who is not only thoroughly alive to their interests, but in close touch with the spirit of the age, and entirely conversant with the wants of a not easily satisfied people."

Although money was tight, the Gardens directors were never ashamed to borrow in order to back Taylor's plans. During 1886 the area around the Grand Conservatory was ripe for improvement. Money was released from the building fund to construct an ornate summer-house in the style of a Chinese Rose Pagoda. The Gardens enormous open-air dancing platform had its entrance enhanced by using a magnificent pair of whales jawbones. Taylor's innovative additions were talking points and drew large crowds – no expense was spared to entice larger, and larger crowds through the turnstiles.

For the 1886 season's entertainment, artists included: Glennies Marionettes; Lillo; Elspa & Echo the flying trapeze artistes; the Beristor Acrobatic Troupe; George Ayton the musician and comedian; Dr. Beauclere and Little Alice magic act; Hector and Victor acrobatic duo; Pongo the Man Monkey and another magician Mr. C.D. Vere. The pinnacle of such illustrious talent was the engagement of an ex soldier from the South Wales Borderers. William Thomas Jones was the proud holder of a Victoria Cross. During 1879 Jones and his fellow Welsh Borderers, under the command of Lieutenants Chard and Bromhead, successfully defended their outpost at Rourkes Drift against an attacking force of 4,000 Zulus. During his appearance in the Gardens Theatre, Jones gave an account of the battle against a fantastic backdrop of the event – painted by the Gardens master painter Mr. Hamilton.

The following season, 1887, was a milestone in the history of the British Royal Family. Queen Victoria had been on the throne for 50 years and the Garden's owners, never short of patriotism, and eye for a marketing opportunity, responded to the royal event by changing the name of the Gardens from Raike's Hall to The Royal Palace Gardens. I decided to contact H. M. Queen's archive at Windsor Castle to see if a formal application had been submitted by the directors to allow them to add the 'Royal' title to the Garden's official name. I was pleased to receive this reply from Windsor's Senior Archivist, Miss Pamela Clark:

"Thank you for your letter of 18 February enquiring about the change of name of Raikes Hall Gardens in Blackpool to the Royal Palace Gardens.

I have made a search of our records in the Royal Archives, but cannot find any reference to these pleasure Gardens.

In fact, applications for the granting of the title 'Royal' were formerly dealt with by the Home Office, so it is in their records in The National Archives that you should seek for records relating to any formal grant of this new title. However, it would be by no means unusual at that period for such a change to have been made without any official permission to do so."

Further enquiries at the National Archives, and Home Office records, also proved fruitless. As Pamela suggested it was not at all unusual, or a serious breach of protocol for institutions to add the 'Royal' to their title in that milestone year of Victoria's Golden Jubilee – indeed it would have been impossible to deter such occurrences and would have seemed rather unpopular in light of the public's patriotic fervour and delight in celebrating the Queen's anniversary.

The Gardens were already popular with the London crowd, and many of the London Sheriffs and other high ranking dignitaries had visited more than once. The Lord Mayor of London, Sir Reginald Hanson, counted the Gardens as one of his favourite holiday centres. The Royal Palace Gardens grandly announced its new status in the following announcement:

"The Royal Palace Gardens are the Palace of Blackpool. Here is to be found enjoyment for all classes. Visitors should not fail to visit this delightful place, five minutes walk from both railway stations and 10 minutes walk from the sea."

Even at this late date and after nearly two decades in operation, the advertising still referred to the Raikes Hall's previous life as a convent! One can only imagine that perhaps it added an extra ingredient of respectability for the history of the place!

By the late 1880s all manner and means of alternative entertainment had been tried at the Royal Palace Gardens. Yet rumours throughout the resort portrayed the Gardens as an economic white elephant. It is true to say it had its financial problems. Nearly twenty thousand pounds was still outstanding from its original mortgage and many hundreds of pounds more was owed to a Preston bank. And yet throughout the 1887 season its turnstiles were busy and masses of visitors enjoyed its pleasures. Many of them came from the annual Lancashire Rifle Volunteer encampment handily set up in a field adjacent to Whitegate Lane (in the area that now has Myrtle and Maple Avenues next to Forest Gate).

Financial issues or not there were new attractions aplenty. The new Monkey House and Aviary, completed for the 1887 season, brought natural history to the masses. It was a haven of colour, especially the feathered section. The building's occupants included White Peacocks, Storks, Laughing Jackasses, Mocking Birds, Russian Jays, Hill Mynahs, Mountain Loreals, John Dyers Parakeets, Kestrels, Hawks, Falcons, Cockatoos, Rose and White Love Birds, Spice Birds, Bishops, Macaws, Eagles, King Parrots, Herons, and a pair of South American Ostriches. On the same animal theme the Seal, Otter and Wild Fowl ponds were very popular. The Otter enclosure first constructed in 1886 originally housed an Otter caught on the River Wyre at St. Michaels.

A complete contrast to the delights of the bird and mammal attractions was the marvelously constructed Gold Room. It's designer and proprietor, Mr. Randall, had put together a true to life exhibition showing a typical working mine, together with a display of full size reproductions of all the largest nuggets found in the goldfields of Australia, New Zealand and the Americas. The display included replicas of the famous Hill End and Welcome Stranger nuggets – infamous for their size alone!

During 1887 the Royal Palace Gardens was the ideal setting for one of the most unusual exhibits – a Japanese village. Created by Mr. Tannacker, it was the only real Japanese village in the land. Tannacker was famous in the art of pseudo-realism, having displayed his creations to much acclaim in Paris, St Petersburg, Dublin and London. The village itself consisted of about 8 dwellings, typically thatched with beaten rice straw.

Another attraction introduced for 1887 was the wonder of mechanical innovation, the switch back railway. Arguably the forerunner of today's white –roller coaster rides. The switchback revolution changed the world of pleasure ground entertainment. It was an idea based on observations by an English man and an American as they toured the gold fields of Arizona. Mr. Stansfield, the owner of the Gardens switchback described it thus:

"The length of the railway will be upwards of 150 yards, consisting of two cars each containing ten persons. They will run in unison. The excitement and exhilaration of switching back cannot be overstated. The traveler no sooner surmounts one elevation to then face another. And at the most sensational point of the whole ride to then descend literally into the bosom of the earth, and forces their way through an overhanging wilderness of rockery and clinging plants!"

The switchback had taken Europe by storm, becoming one of the most sought after pastimes of the era patronised by many members of the British Royal family along with foreign monarchs and princes.

During the 1888 season, Stansfield introduced the sensational Aerial Flight to the Royal Palace Gardens which was often described as the original overhead cable car. It gave riders the thrill of balloon flights without the dangers. However, in September 1888 the contraption had its first accident. Professor Dexter, an illusionist appearing at the Gardens, gave a graphic account of the tragic drama:

"I was standing on the grand terrace, and was casually watching the overhead car. The cable suddenly went slack, and the car and its occupants were dashed with great force against the ornamental wall of the terrace, almost at the centre of the open air picture. I immediately ran to the spot and seeing several people hurt and some were bleeding. I dispatched several cabbies to fetch some doctors."

Luckily the accident looked more serious than it actually was. There were no fatalities although many of the occupants suffered facial cuts and injuries and also broken legs and arms.

Manchester artist Edwin Firth had throughout his professional career painted many outdoor scenic masterpieces, and yet his 1889 Commission for the Royal Palace Gardens eclipsed his previous work. City of Canton became his most celebrated and admired work. It's tremendous size, being some 50 feet in height and a length that encompassed 12,000 square feet meant that it had to be assembled, not in the traditional site in the Gardens below the grand terrace, but in a new location adjacent to the trotting track. The painting's intimate scenes, if any thing so vast could be intimate, were based on the Chinese War of 1856, and brought to life the battles with the added pyrotechnic effects by the Gardens own firework master, Mr. Cooper. Complementing the scenic work and the firework displays were realistic military maneuvers by 150 local school children all knitted out in authentic uniforms and regalia.

> Mr. Stansfield has forwarded us the following letter:—
>
> *To the Editor.*
>
> Sir,—Lest you should have received an erroneous account of to-day's accident and its cause, I beg to give you the facts.
>
> The sole cause of the accident was the breaking of an iron shackle which fitted over one of the anchor posts at south end.
>
> On inspection it proves to have been a flaw in the iron which caused the fracture. One end of the main cable being thus set free the car descended rapidly in an oblique direction to the ground, and in so doing came in contact with the wall which projects towards the picture at the centre of the terrace. Had there been no wall there would have been no serious injury done to any of the passengers, as the car would simply have run along the ground upon the wheels fixed in the base of it.
>
> I am pleased to hear that one gentleman only is seriously injured—his leg being broken — and that he is already progressing favourably.
>
> Hoping you will favour me by giving publicity to these facts,—I remain, Yours most respectfully,
>
> J. D. STANSFIELD,
> Royal Palace Gardens,
> Blackpool.
> September 10th, 1888.

On the music from for the 1889 season, the Royal Palace Garden's regulars, the Guards Band, were joined that year by Herr Hofffman's Orchestra whose conducting skills and enthusiasm, and his rousing military style, was possibly linked by the fact that the orchestra members, mostly of German origin, couldn't wait for the season's end so they could return to the fatherland!

A complete contrast to the eccentricities of the Hoffman Orchestra was the stability of the rival Gardens adjacent. John Hodgson had for more than three decades controlled the turbulent fortunes of the Belle Vue Strawberry Gardens. Layton born Hodgson began his career at the old Whitegate Lane coaching house, the No 3. Here in the 1860s Hodgson, in partnership with John Noblet created the original Belle Vue Gardens, but during 1864 they moved further down Whitegate Lane to establish the Albert Hotel. Within months they refurbished the Albert, renaming it the Belle Vue Strawberry Gardens.

During 1870 Hodgson set aside a small fortune to build a Belle Vue Music Hall within the grounds. The building was nearly completed when a mystery fire engulfed the ornate timber structure. Rumour and suspicions were rife – as was the gossip about the cause of the fire! The police viewed it as a malicious act by a person or persons unknown. Sadly Hodgson had not insured the building. The replacement cost was in excess of £500, but with typical fortitude he and his partner soldiered on to establish one of the most famous watering holes in Blackpool's history – one that continues to this day, long after the demise of its famous neighbour and rival the Royal Palace Gardens.

Small as these images are, they are worth including. The image above shows the carriage drive that ran parallel to Whitegate Lane between Hornby Road and Devonshire Square. The High-Wire for Blondin's act is clearly visible with the Fairy Fountain in the foreground. Circa. 1880s

Below is an image of the lake and the Grandstand overlooking the sports field – the Grand Opera House can be seen behind the stand.

Chapter 8

PROGRESS &
FOUNDERS EARLY DEATH

The Royal Palace Gardens and Blackpool had come a long way from their humble beginnings. During 1811 Blackpool's resident population numbered a mere 580 rising steadily to 20,000 by 1889. Although the growth of the population was fairly gradual the influx of seasonal visitors was rising rapidly year-on-year.

Better communications, especially rail travel, arguably influenced the enthusiasm for the resort. By 1863 Blackpool has become a leading northern spa town, competing with the more up market resorts of Scarborough, Southport and Llandudno. Nevertheless its yearly visitors numbered some 134,000 rising to an enormous 700,000 by 1869 – topping the 1 million mark by 1889. Pretty impressive growth for any resort and the best was yet to come.

Blackpool had by this time constructed three railway terminals, named North, Central and South Stations respectively, which catered for the thousands of visitors. On their arrival they enjoyed the convenience of over 300 registered Landaus and scores of horse-drawn wagons to convey them to various destinations of pleasure in the resort. Complementing the horse-drawn transportation was the mechanical marvel of the Victorian age: the electric tram car! The novelty, and thus popularity of this mode of pleasure transport was demonstrated in 1889 when the figures for one week showed that 42,000 passengers paid their 2d for the two and a half mile journey along the promenade.

Initially visitors were drawn to Blackpool for its healthy air, therapeutic sea water, safe bathing beaches and magical sunsets. Thousands were accommodated by the historical forerunner of the Bed & Breakfast

establishments known as 'the company house', where visitors brought their own food. This was cooked and served by the landlady. Guests even had to bring their own cruets!

Blackpool's natural assets were complimented by its many man-made attractions. The piers were in full swing offering numerous steamer excursions to Barrow, Southport and Llandudno. Pleasure craft by the score plied their trade from the golden sands. Arguably heading the resort's cultural aspirations was the resplendent Winter Gardens and it's near neighbour and rival The Royal Palace Gardens. These entertainment Meccas were headed by two characters with flair and innovative talents. In control of the new Winter Gardens complex was William Holland, who through his efforts in the local charity scene was aptly referred to as the "People's William". Likewise his counterpart at the Royal Palace Gardens, George Bart Taylor was held in the highest of regards by both visitors and locals alike. To be fair to Taylor, his working budget fell far short of his entertainment rival at the Winter Gardens and yet with guile and enterprise he managed to attract huge crowds.

Taylor's interest in sport was mirrored in the Gardens recreational activities. He encouraged the harness racing, or trotting, fraternity to hold regular meets on the ground's oval track. Cricket was in his blood and he purposely went out of his way to develop and encourage the newly formed Blackpool Cricket Club. The Gardens thus took on an international flavour with a visit in 1889 of an England Cricket eleven team.

Taylor was an advocate of the power of advertising. With the introduction of the trams he had taken out the option on the advertising space to promote the Royal Palace Gardens. Taylor's first love was in the field of variety theatre. With limited resources he constantly engaged acts of quality. One of the highest paid artistes in the history of the Gardens appeared in 1889. Ace balloonist Captain Whelan of Sheffield demanded £50 per night to perform his act that was built around his 20,000 cubic foot balloon named Victoria. Whelan's assistant was the daring parachutist John Whitely. However, Whelan's act was often cancelled, the trouble caused by Blackpool Gas Company failing to supply gas because of his unpaid bills.

The sudden death of George Bartholomew Taylor made headlines and shocked the town to its core. His funeral created more public interest than that some years earlier of Blackpool's visionary Enoch Read – Reads Avenue is named after him to this day. Taylor's funeral embraced all the social classes. Hundreds of mourners including the largest gathering of Freemasons, numbering some 57, attended the internment at Layton Cemetery. The plain pitch pine coffin, made by Wards Bonney of Raikes Hill, bore the simple inscription:

"George Bart Taylor, died May 29th 1890 aged 36 years."

His life may have been short but his energy and enthusiasm, matched by his remarkable achievements, were great. His most incredible legacy was the Royal Palace Gardens and its entertainment and sporting ethos. Sadly gone today, ironic then that the only thing remaining is his grave – even that is rarely visited or acknowledged more than a century later. His short life is worth recording here as a mark of respect to a man that made Blackpool in those early pioneering days – a true Victorian entrepreneur.

As a youngster of twelve, Taylor came to live with his uncle George Ormerod at Newton Hall. His early school days were associated with Bambers Collegiate in Adelaide Street, and at Dommon's South Shore High School. His early working life was spent as a clerk at Talbot Road Railway Station (Blackpool North Station). As a young man he initially moved to Liverpool where he opened an Hotel. Around 1879 he married Jennie Ann Ward of Newton Lodge, Staining, and for a few years he and his wife ran a millinery shop in Cookson Street. On his majority (aged 21) he became a full time director of the Raikes Hall Company.

Through the years that followed he invested steadily in the Raikes financial future and yet in 1880 the seemingly prosperous Raikes Complex almost folded, beset by financial difficulties. The companies response to this troubled period was to appoint Taylor as Company Secretary and Manager. His enthusiastic approach and enterprising methods initiated a complete reversal in the companies financial fortunes, it's future decidedly rosier under his guidance.

Throughout his career Taylor was linked with many Blackpool enterprises. He was director of the Blackpool Aquarium Company, the Royal Hotel Company, and the much maligned Lane Ends Estate. His out of town interests included the ownership of land in Morecambe and he was also a shareholder in a small theatre in Wigan.

Taylor was mourned but the Gardens continued as he would have wanted them to. He loved innovation and drama, so would have been delighted by the next marvel that would literally light up the Gardens as never before. The illuminations would set a precedent that Blackpool would build on and expand as the years went by – but the seeds were sown first at the Royal Palace Gardens.

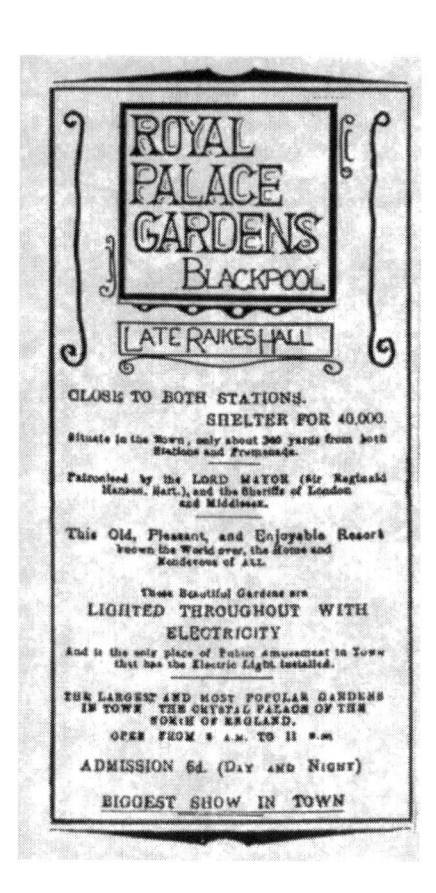

This advert proudly displays the new name of the Gardens with the 'Royal' prefix. It also advertises the fact that the Gardens are the first attraction in Blackpool to be illuminated with electric light – the precursor to the famous illuminations that developed later in the resort.

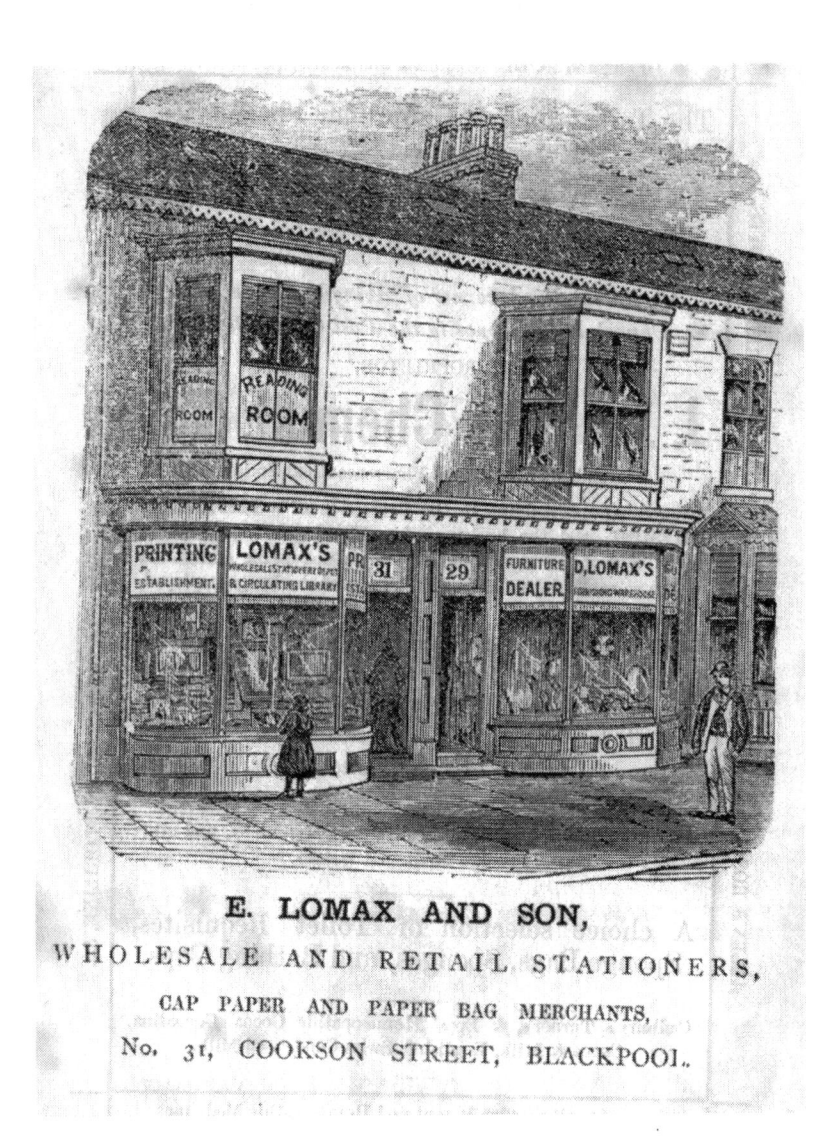

E. LOMAX AND SON,
WHOLESALE AND RETAIL STATIONERS,
CAP PAPER AND PAPER BAG MERCHANTS,
No. 31, COOKSON STREET, BLACKPOOL.

Local businesses happily advertised in the Gardens. This advert was in the guidebook and shows a local stationary shop.

Chapter 9

LET THERE BE ELECTRIC ILLUMINATION!

Despite the depth of feelings towards Taylor's sudden death, his colleagues and friends at the Royal Palace Gardens appointed long-time associate Charles Iddeson as the Gardens new acting manager. Peter Ward, Taylor's brother-in-law, became Iddeson's assistant. Taylor was to miss one of the most exciting periods in the Gardens colourful history – the installation of the Victorian era's scientific marvel: electricity!

The wonder of electric light had reached Blackpool in the late 1870s and was finally introduced to the Royal Palace Gardens in 1891. The intervening years has seen it become more widely available and most importantly more affordable. The electrical system chosen by the Gardens directorship was that of the Edison – Swann Company. The same firm had carried out major contracts at Manchester's Victoria Station and Palace Theatre, and overseas in Port Said, New York and Berlin.

In April and May of 1891, electrical engineers by the dozen arrived at the Royal Palace Gardens where they proceeded to install a 54 horse power engine supplied by Musgroves of Bolton. Local builder Mr. W. Eaves (another local with a street named after him) built the Dynamo house. The Gardens became Blackpool's first entertainment centre to be lit by electric light.

The brilliance of the electrical supply was matched by the efforts of acting manager, Iddeson. He personally supervised the extensive alterations carried out through the 1891 season. The ornate ballroom was completely refurbished, with the artistic work being carried out by top Canadian landscape artist Captain Loxton Rawbone. He painted realistic views of the

Niagara River and its celebrated falls on the ballroom walls. The equally popular Indian Village constructed some years earlier was also completely renovated. Here the patrons could relax in comfortable chairs and take in the strains of an orchestra, or watch the clever performances of athletes and jugglers and a raised Dias

During the 1891 season the Forest Aviary with its colourful collection of rare birds from around the world was as popular as ever. Along with the variety and music hall acts – the quality matched the excellence of previous seasons. The company engaged at great expense Mrs. Hunts celebrated Ladies Orchestra (Les Militiare). The gifted Lennon Family also returned for the season and Eddison's invention, the phonograph, was a popular exhibit. The speciality of that season was the exhibition of Sir Noel Patons marvelous fairy picture 'Midsummer Eve'. The variety and quality of the attractions emphasised the motto of the Royal Palace Gardens, that stated proudly:

"No where in the world can so much be seen for so little! Admission 6d"

Throughout its history, the Royal Palace Gardens and its predecessor the Raikes Hall Gardens continued to play a leading role in the horticultural aspirations of the Fylde Coast, and by the 1890s Gardening connoisseurs by the hundred flocked there. The Gardens horticultural displays had also developed over time and their centre piece was the 500 yard round conservatory, a masterpiece of Victorian glass work that enclosed a wealth of floral magnificence. Mr. Houghton, the head Gardener, and his enthusiastic staff, had the conservatory display in grand order. The palms, rubber plants, and tropical foliage, together with a rare New Zealand plant 'Dicksons Antartica' created much interest. Away from the heat and humidity of the tropical area, the shaded fern era offered a cool and delightful retreat. The charm of the Fern House, so popular in Victorian times, was enhanced by waterfalls streaming over moss and lichen covered boulders.

As a contrast to the peace and tranquility of the floral exhibits were the grounds other attractions. The switchback railway, aerial car, skating rink, boating lake, camera obscure, photographic gallery, a model of Shakespeare's birth place, the great Whales jaw bones, a handsome billiard saloon containing five tables, seal pond, the monkey house and Aviary, and the more than unusual Peruvian Mummy, reputed to be a 4,000 year old Inca Princess.

On July 15th 1893 the Royal Palace Gardens opened a new cycle track along with a new variety theatre – the Opera House – that cost the company the large sum of £1,421 14shillings and 4pence. The Gardens had always appealed to the dancing and theatre fraternity and these new attractions added another dimension to the Gardens attraction for the public. This was confirmed by the many cycle enthusiasts who started to visit and use this facility. Hundreds of fans attended a capital cycling tournament on September 9th 1893. The prestigious event attracted many of the countries premier racers. Top of the bill was a five mile handicap race with a first prize of £3 and a second and third prize of £1 and 10 shillings respectively. Preston's Mr. R. Cookson walked away with the first prize.

In addition the popular horse trotting track had an immense following, and as many as 5,000 equine fans attended weekly meetings. The sports minded manager of the Gardens, Charles Iddeson, actively encouraged many Blackpool clubs to compete on the grounds extensive sporting facilities where cricket, football, bowling and other games were well established. With the companies blessing Iddeson allocated even more funds to the development of the sporting facilities in order to make money out of the events.

On the face of it the Gardens seemed to thrive, the Whitsuntide fortnight figures for 1893 showed that over 200,000 people poured through the turnstiles – far exceeding that of any other Blackpool entertainment venue of the time.

The new Opera House theatre was an immense success, the 3pm matinee and 7pm evening performances attracting hundreds of theatre-goers. Some of the major shows that 1893 season included artistes like Jenny Valmore (the people's idol), direct from London's music halls Miss Marie De Simencourt (ballad vocalist), Monsieur Essman (equilibrist and juggler), the Velones (acrobats) with musical direction under the baton of Mr. Wilkinson. The undoubted scoop of the season was none other than the darling of the English stage, 25 year old Katie Laurence who, although described in variety articles as a serio comic, possessed a fine singing voice too. Miss Laurence appeared at the Royal Palace Gardens just 16 hours after a successful engagement at London's famous Alhambra Theatre. Her speciality was an enchanting rendition of Daisy Bell often described as the cyclists national anthem – dedicated to the pedal cyclists of America. Although Katie was a married lady, her good looks and endearing charm produced a throng of gentleman admirers who sent her love letters wherever she performed.

"Daisy, Daisy give me your answer do
I'm half crazy, hopeful in love with you
It won't be a stylish marriage
I can't afford a carriage
But you look sweet upon the street
On a bicycle built for two!

We will go tandem as man and wife
Daisy, Daisy
Peddling our way down the road of life
I and my daisy bell
When the roads and we both despise
Please men the lambs as well
There are bright lights in those dazzling ice
A beautiful daisy bell

Daisy, Daisy give me your answer do
I'm half crazy, hopeful in love with you
It won't be a stylish marriage
I can't afford a carriage
But you look sweet upon the street
On a bicycle built for two!"

The great outdoor feature at the Gardens in 1893 was W.H. Dugans great scenic painting 'Copenhagen'. In front of which, at precisely 9.30pm every night a flare signified that hostilities were about to begin in Copenhagen Bay and after a minute or so the firing, bayoneting and the sinking of battle ships was realistically reenacted for a thrilled audience. Thousands witnessed this spectacle and the firework display that followed.

From London's music hall royalty to spectacular dramas played out in front of their very eyes, the Victorian visitors to the Royal Palace Gardens never left disappointed and always bursting with stories and memories to share once back home. None could have imagined that the Gardens days were numbered and that dark clouds were gathering to threaten its future and very existence.

Royal Palace Gardens

ROYAL PALACE GARDENS
BLACKPOOL.
GENERAL MANAGER & SECRETARY - CHAS. IDDESON.

PROFESSOR MORRITT
ENGAGED AT ENORMOUS EXPENSE,
DIRECT FROM THE ROYAL AQUARIUM.
Who will introduce his
"FLYING LADY."
The Most Astounding Aerial Phenomenon of the Day.

GRAND OVATION GIVEN TO THE G.O.M.

BLONDIN.

EXTRAORDINARY ENTHUSIASM.
VOCIFEROUS APPLAUSE FROM THOUSANDS OF SPECTATORS.
THE MOST MARVELLOUS SHOW ON EARTH.
NEARLY 80 YEARS OF AGE.

More to be seen here for 6d. than at any other place of Amusement in the World. JUDGE FOR YOURSELVES.

> Of all the sights in England now,
> And I've looked everywhere,
> There is not one of any sort,
> With Blondin can compare;
> He is the marvel of his age –
> That everyone admits –
> So *fit* it is that he should beat
> All others into *fits*:
>
> The world counts seven Wonders up
> An eighth I will install,
> The Hero of Niagara,
> And greatest of them all.
>
> Though small in stature, slight in build,
> With truth it may be said,
> He's never *undersized* but when
> You see him *overhead*,
> A tripping of his own ac*cord*
> Like some fantastic elf
> To whom is given *rope* enough
> But not to *hang* himself.

BLONDIN — MASTER OF THE HIGH WIRE

The world famous Blondin impresses the crowds at the Royal Palace Gardens with his high wire act. He drew large crowds and the Niagara Café and exhibition was created to compliment his seasonal appearances.

Chapter 10

ENTERTAINMENT RIVALS

Blackpool's growing reputation as a leading resort of pleasure was enhanced by a more than favourable press. Even the national press echoed the merits of Blackpool in general and the Royal Palace Gardens in particular. A London editor wrote:

"To go to Blackpool and not visit the Royal Palace Gardens is to visit London and not visit the Crystal Palace or Westminster Abbey, or go to Rome and not visit the Vatican or the Coliseum!"

Even before the famous tower was constructed, the Blackpool entertainment scene had plenty to offer Victorian guests. Those Victorian engineering masterpieces the piers entertained the sea front masses. The North Pier, mainly for leisurely promenading; the South Pier (now Central Pier) had more shops and stalls and amusements; Victoria Pier (now South Pier), like its neighbour catered for amusements rather than dignified promenading. However, they all developed thriving summer entertainments and soon had theatres playing twice nightly and popular artistes who were more than happy to spend a couple of months every summer in one venue, rather than the rigours of touring, with regular work. The resorts leading hotels in clouding the County and Lane Ends (now Harry Ramsdens), Bailey's Hotel (now the Metropole) and the Clifton Hotel at Talbot Square and Promenade, also provided regular seasonal entertainments.

In its early years Blackpool was initially a renowned bathing spa town, and it capitalized on the 19th Century phenomena of the indoor swimming pool. The resort's main offerings were the magnificent plunge pools and baths of

Reads Baths, Cocker Street Baths and the promenades palatial Prince of Wales Baths.

Blackpool's cultural aspirations were provided for by the many assembly rooms and theatres, including the original Borough Theatre – later Feldman's and then the Queens Theatre – situated on what is now the site of TK Max. The Prince of Wales Theatre and the small yet magnificent bijou Theatre Royal both situated in Talbot Square.

Blackpool's much maligned Strawberry Gardens at the Belle Vue Hotel, the Number 3 (formerly the Didsbury Hotel), the Oxford Hotel and the semi-rural Cherry Tree Hotel and Gardens attracted visitors by the thousands, and each of these entertainment and recreational attractions, as time went by, represented a direct threat to the economic viability of the Royal Palace Gardens. Yet arguably the biggest threat came in the shape of the superb Church Street complex known as the Winter Gardens. Included within the Winter Gardens facilities was a new Opera House, skating rink, indoor Gardens, Indian room, variety theatre and dance halls. It was also within walking distance of both the North and Central train stations. All this was certainly a blow to the Royal Palace Gardens and turned out to be competition it struggled to compete with.

Seemingly unperturbed by the ever increasing competition, the Royal Palace Garden's directors tried even harder to link mass pleasure with economic stability. During the 1894 season Charles Iddeson approved plans for the construction of the Niagara building. The octagonal structure housed an enormous cycloramic painting, by the French artist Phillipoteaux, that would cost an enormous amount. For the construction of the building and then fitting it out as a cafe, along with the cycloramic painting, was in the region of £3,628.14s 4d.

The company engaged an old military campaigner, a Captain Lacy, to guide the visitors through the wonders of the Niagara Exhibition. Many people had heard about the Niagara Falls through newspaper stories but few, if any, had actually been able to see the falls for themselves as travel around the world was too expensive for working people. This exhibition and cafe at the Royal Palace Gardens was the next best thing and the huge cyclorama painting gave a realistic impression in terms of size and scale. The Blackpool Gazette described the new attraction thus:

"Niagara is now open and a more magnificent sight of the kind we have never seen. The whole is one immense circular picture which goes around the entire building. The spectators stand on a high platform in the centre, and the picture is so well executed that the illusion is most complete. Below are prettily laid out walks which are made to resemble those on the picture, and it is impossible to say where the reality is or where the picture commences. The Niagara Falls, the boats, the bridge, the scenery and the visitors are all minutely depicted and one can easily fancy being within a few yards of the great Niagara Falls. By all means see Niagara. Mr. Iddeson is to be congratulated on having added another splendid show to the sights of Blackpool."

Although Charles Iddeson's entertainment ideas were more than popular with the Royal Palace Gardens patrons, they were nevertheless costly to create and maintain. The Niagara exhibition had to be housed in an expensive octagonal building. Its construction costs became a great financial burden on the Garden's already depleted resources. Even so, the 1895 season began with its popular Whitsun week opening ceremony.

But there were storm clouds on the horizon. In reality Blackpool's alternative centres of entertainment were having a distinctly negative effect on the Royal Palace Gardens attendance figures. Many of the patrons were being lured away by the quality and variety, and amusements, available in William Holland's Winter Gardens complex. Also the resorts new 'wonder of the world' and engineering marvel the Blackpool Tower had much to offer for a more demanding and discerning public. It's splendid Pavilion and Macham designed ballroom with their polished wood floors and plush carpets had a more luxurious feel than the bare boards and coconut matting at the Royal Palace Gardens. In spite of this, the directors backed Iddeson's determination and enthusiasm to keep the Gardens open.

Over the years the most renowned variety artistes has graced the various stages at the Royal Palace Gardens. In the early 1890s London's "Prince of Comedians", Gus Elen had graced the stage and during the 1880s the world's most expensive act, John Holturn, appeared at the Gardens. Despite the misgivings of the general public, the 1895 summer season was to prove the most expensive and arguably the most interesting in the grounds history.

Opening the season was none other than the King of the Rifle, Captain Fowler. Crack shot Fowler's 1895 appearance at the Gardens was a unique event in Blackpool' colourful entertainment history. Fowler introduced the resorts visitors and residents alike to the thrill of clay pigeon shooting. He was a larger than life character with many a tale to tell. He told his story through the pages of the Blackpool Times. Some years before, in the 1880s, Fowler was based in Africa during the troubles with Lobengula – King of the Matables – and was offered a great deal of money by Cecil Rhodes to fight as a mercenary against the African Chieftan. Fowler wisely turned down the lucrative offer and instead threw his lot in with Africa's great theatrical agent Luscombe Suarelle. Fowler was paid £140 per month for his sharp shooting skills and exploits. His travels took him to twenty five countries where his performances were witnessed by rich travelers, English nobility and the Prince of Wales, Tsar of Russia, Sultan of Turkey, Khedive of Egypt and the Shah of Persia. During his time in North America he served as a scout with the infamous Indian fighter, Major Frank North. The adventures with North led to the loss of two of Fowler's fingers on his left hand, as a result of an unfortunate encounter with members of the Bannoch tribe. Fowler had a companion at the Royal Palace Gardens engagement, none other than the lady champion shot of the world Miss Nellie Frazell. They had previously appeared together at London's Crystal Palace.

One of the outstanding features of the 1895 season was the marvellous condition of the Royal Palace Gardens. Head Gardener, Mr. Woodcock, and his team of green fingered helpers, had worked miracles with the ground's shrubberies, flower beds, Ferneries and the contents of the luscious tropical conservatory.

One man-made attraction which created much public interest during the season was the giant Fairy Fountain. Built in 1893 and costing some £2,000, it was the brain child of Charles Iddeson. It was situated on the site of the giant outdoor painting just below the Grand Terrace, bordering Whitegate Lane (now Whitegate Drive). The Gardens ornamental lake, through a specially constructed pump house, supplied the 100,000 gallons of water per hour needed for the fountains 190 jets. The fountain was a wonderful spectacle at night when illuminated by hundreds of electric lamps.

In the Niagara building the popular cafe had been completely refurbished. Mr. Duggan, the master internal designer, had tastefully covered the cafe walls in peacock blue with nice bordered ornamentation. The roof panels were stenciled freehand with trophies representing Canada and America. Adjacent to the cafe was a more than comfortable lounge area, and here Dugan painted the walls with continuous canvasses depicting mountainous peaks. Nestling within these panoramic painted scenes was one representing a Native Bazzaar. One view in particular captured the public's attention, that of Balar Hissar at Cabul. The fine piece of work was of particular interest to the visitors as it coincided with a visit of the Ameer of Afganhistan's son, Prince Nasrullah, to England as a guest of Queen Victoria.

Another major attraction of the Gardens 1895 season was Professor Morrit and his man in a trance act. The great illusionist had drawn unprecedented crowds to the Royal Aquarium in London. Patrons, particularly those in the musical field, had paid the startling sum of a pound per seat. The Royal Palace Gardens management notified the local Blackpool press that Morrit's act was the most expensive in the resort's entertainment history!

Two of the South's most talented artists graced the Royal Palace Gardens Opera House and other stages during the season. From the London Pavilion came serio and dancer Miss Nellie Stratton. Also Middlesex funny man Mark Sheridan. Popular performer Professor Howard who for over 20 years choreographed the pseudo battle scenes in front of the giant outdoor painting showed his dexterity by appearing in the 1895 season as an illusionist. His act included the sand trick, The Queen of Koe, and the Vanishing Lady Phenomena. Direct from the Folies Bergere in Paris, and the London Empire came Miss Holtum (daughter of the cannon King) the first and only lady juggler in the world. Other contemporary Royal Palace acts included the Three Acroes billed as 'The Funny Knockabouts!', the Sisters Philips, the Bothers Lorenzi, Minnie Mario the serio comic, Lottie Lennox the Lavender Girl, Master George Elliot (Little Chip) and Grace Lloyd – sister of the more famous Marie Lloyd.

Seemingly the most popular, if not most sensational act of the 1895 season, was Jean Francios Gravalet who was known around the world as the famous Blondin. Some months prior to Blondin's Blackpool visit rumours were circulated throughout the resort that this Blondin was a counterfeit or imposter and not the real one at all. As a result thousands of visitors flocked to the Gardens to witness for themselves. After seeing Blondin's thrilling, open air, high wire act, they were left in no doubt that they had seen the real thing. This publicity preceded the Great Blondin's appearances at the Gardens:

"Of all the sights in England now,
And I've looked everywhere,
There is not one of any sort,
With Blondin can compare;
He is the marvel of his age –
That everyone admits –
So fit it is that he should beat
All others into fits.

The world counts seven wonders up
An eighth I will install,
The Hero of Niagara,
And greatest of them all.

Though small in stature, slight in build,
With truth it might be said,
He's never undersized but when
You see him overhead,
A tripping of his own accord
Like some fantastic elf
To whom is given rope enough
But not to hang himself!"

Blondin billed as being 80 years of age (perhaps the reason for the rumours and disbelief that an elderly man could perform such an act) but his actual age was 71 – to add to his woes, he was suffering from quite a severe back problem. In fact during his last performance at the Royal Palace Gardens in August of 1895, he had to be helped down from the high wire and taken, under supervision of a doctor, back to his accommodation at the Talbot Hotel. Here he gradually recovered his health, ably nursed by a 25 year old chambermaid Miss James. In gratitude to Miss James the grand old man married her some months later.

During that year of 1895, a sad death occurred suddenly taking everyone by surprise. The Winter Gardens designer William Holland passed away on 29th December. The Royal Palace Gardens also ended the year with a tragedy. There was an unfortunate accident when a section of the boundary wall at the extreme end of Raikes Parade collapsed without warning and buried two workmen. Christopher Trainor of Vicarage Lane, Marton and Benjamin Price of Oddfellow Street were the men in question. Sadly the latter, Price, was killed.

The greatest misfortune for the Royal Palace Gardens came in the form of the end of year accounts when, once again, despite Herculean efforts by staff and directors alike, the books again showed a loss for in excess of £2,200. Try as they might, the outstanding debts, in particular that owed to the many money lenders, was a tremendous burden. The directors were attempting to alter the constitution to allow them to sell off surplus land. There was no other choice.

History of Raikes Hall

Royal Palace Gardens

Royal Palace Gardens
Blackpool — *Late Raikes Hall*

Grand Opera House, Football Ground & Lake

Opposite image shows the scale of the outside diorama used as a backdrop to the battle of Alexandria reenactment at the Gardens. They even had a sinking ship to add to the spectacle for audiences. Sign to right advertises seats for 2d!

The performance finale ended with spectacular firework diplays – many local volunteers also worked as extras.

During the day these huge outdoor painted scenes were enjoyed by those either on foot – or in their horse and carriages as they drove through the gardens – stopping off for refreshments at bars and cafe's available in the grounds.

Image Copyright: Johnston Press Ltd
Used with permission.

Many scenes were painted of current conflicts at the Royal Palace Gardens for battle reenactments – like this one that depicts the Khyber Pass during the Afghan War.

Chapter 11

ROYAL PALACE GARDENS FOR SALE

By 1896 the majority of the Royal Palace Gardens directors who favoured certain amendments to the companies constitution had their way. Not only did the changes allow for the sale of surplus land, it also gave provision, if the price was right, for the sale of the whole estate. With this in mind the directors placed the resplendent Gardens on the open property market. There was a tremendous public interest, in particular from a group of local land speculators. On the 13th July 1896 a syndicate headed by financial wizard, and owner of the Tower and Winter Gardens, purchased the Royal Palace Gardens lock stock and barrel for £79,965, 10s 8d. About the same time, by pure coincidence, two of the Gardens main entertainment rivals were also sold including the adjacent Belle Vue Strawberry Gardens for £16,000 along with Talbot Road's Theatre Royal for £29,000.

John Bickerstaff knew what he was doing when he headed the consortium that purchased the rival Royal Palace Gardens. After the money he had invested in building the tower and also running the piers, along with the Winter Gardens complex, he needed to make sure that no rival entertainment venue would attract the crowds away from his main interests. The 1896 season at the Royal Palace Gardens continued, although under a much tighter financial constraints than before under this new management.

However, the writing was on the wall. However, the artistes and attractions previously booked were honoured.

Highlights of the 1896 season was a first for Blackpool with the appearance at the Gardens of the engineering marvel the motor car! Proud owner, Liverpool's Mr. Milliner exhibited his 1896 Benz after its initial appearance at London's Crystal Palace.

For most of that season there was much behind the scenes activity within the Gardens directorship. As a result, there was the emergence of a new company. On the 25th January 1897, with a capital standing at £60,000 in £10 shares, the Raikes Hall Estate Company Ltd was born. The principal shareholders were John Bickerstaff (Tower Company), J. Nickson (Talbot Road), F. Nickson (Station Hotel), T. Blaine (Burnley), R.B. Mather (Hornby Road), D. Kemp (Blackburn), and John Kemp (Great Harwood). The number of directors was to be no less than five, or more than eleven. In addition to those mentioned, other major subscribers were: T. Sergenson, J. Lee, C. Iddeson, and G.L. Seed. Almost to a man the new directorship was unanimous in the decision to sell the Royal Palace Garden's surplus land. It was a necessity to balance the books and repay debts.

The grand sale was organized to take place at Blackpool's Albion Hotel, conducted by the resorts top auctioneer Mr. T Carter. With such an opportunity to buy prime coastal land, the attendance was good, with many of Blackpool's leading visionaries looking for a bargain. Manchester solicitor Mr. J. C. Walker read out the conditions of the land sale. One clause of particular interest was one that stipulated that no shops could be erected on the said land, apart from a designated plot on the corner of Whitegate Lane (now Whitegate Drive) and Raikes Road (now Church Street at the Number 3 Hotel end). Generous parcels of land were sold, including 3,408 square yards on the east side of Raikes Parade which was purchased by a Mr. Hargreaves for 17 shillings and 6d per square yard. Mr. J. H. Robinson paid the same price per square yard for 3,220 yards fronting Raikes Parade. The most expensive plot was a stretch of land opposite the Number 3 Hotel, comprising of about 1,248 square yards – sold to Mr. Hargreaves at 24 shillings per square yard. Overall the sale raised in excess of £15,000.

It was interesting to note that one of the last functions of the old Royal Palace Gardens company was a social and dance for the benefit of Professor Howard, a renowned dance master, illusionist and master of ceremonies. Howard had been associated with, and frequently performed at the grounds since the early 1870s.

The new company, Raikes Hall Estates, continued to support local organized sports, in particular Blackpool Football Club, who played all their home matches at the Gardens, despite the ground at times resembling what one wit described as "an African watering hole".

The decline of the Gardens was now underway. Sections of land were sold off for house building and the estate began to contract inwards towards the original Regency Raikes Hall. During the next four years the entire complex would be sold off and its buildings demolished or sold. The Niagara building and café was sold and transported to Rigby Road at the promenade end. There is was reconstructed on a new site but as a roller skating rink. Thus it remained for many years until the structure began to become unstable due to it age many years later. Many had forgotten its origins by then and the impact it had on the public when it first opened.

The auction catalogue for the Gardens makes fascinating reading and is worth reproducing here to understand the sheer scale and quality of the fixtures on offer. Many of them would be reused in Backpool's other attractions and interestingly the Indian Pavilion and Indian Lounge, and Royal Opera House would be names that continued in other areas of the resort ones the originals had ceased to exist at what was the Royal Palace Gardens.

The plot of land held on the south side of Hornby Road was the first to be sold off and is therefore not listed inn the catalogue. After the terms of sale notice, and indicating that the three plots were to be sold as freehold, the catalogue very descriptively sets out the following main Lots for sale:

Lot 1:

The ORNAMENTAL SEAL POND with centre fountains is situate opposite to the northerly entrance of the GRAND OPERA HOUSE.

There is a GRAND STAND overlooking the racecourse, bicycle track, football field, and cricket field, and capable of seating 700 people. Large football and cricket field, and also a recently laid bicycle track and racecourse. On the north side of the football field, there is ANOTHER GRAND STAND capable of holding 1,500 persons, with fully licensed bar and good dressing rooms thereunder.

In the grounds there is an ORNAMENTAL LAKE with well wooded islands. This lake is used for boating, and is also well stocked with fish.

A large MONKEY HOUSE, fitted with heating apparatus and other appliances; also, the STABLES adjoining the same.

A fine CONSERVATORY, FERNERIES, and SKATING RINK, all under one roof.

The OCTAGONAL BUILDING with large CAFÉ and Refreshment Room adjoining, lighted throughout with electric light, and containing the famous cycloramic picture of NIAGARA FALLS, painted by Phillipotaux, the great French Artist.

Near to the Niagara Building is the OLD BALL ROOM now used as a FANCY FAIR, with Blacksmiths', Carpenters', Joiners', and other Workshops and Stables in the rear.

Opposite thereto are the ENGINE HOUSE and ELECTRIC LIGHT WORKS, brick built and lined with glazed bricks, and fitted with Steam Engines, Boilers, and other Appliances as set out in the list of fixtures.

A LARGE OPEN-AIR DANCING FLOOR with Band Stand and Grand Stand overlooking same, and TWO FULLY LICENSED SERVING BARS attached, the latter of handsome design and substantially built of brick and stone.

The Magistrates' permission to sell intoxicating liquors extends to three temporary bars in various parts of the Gardens, which can be used when required, on such occasions as Agricultural Shows, Sports, &c.

In the magnificently laid out ITALIAN GARDENS is a grand ILLUMINATED FAIRY FOUNTAIN situated in the center, ejecting water to a height of 100 feet. A well laid cinder track, well adapted for athletic training purposes, running the whole length from North to South, and situate in the Eastern part of the Gardens.

LARGE TOMATO and PROPOGATING HOUSES, also LARGE and WELL-STOCKED VINERIES.

The whole of the Gardens and Estate is fringed with fine healthy trees and shrubs, and a substantial boundary wall encloses the same. The Gardens are approached by a magnificent Four-arch Main Entrance in Church Street, surmounted with Electric Light of 6,000 Candle Power, and standing 100 feet high. There are also additional entrances from Raikes Road and Hornby Road, with the necessary Lodges, Gardener's Cottage, &c. The site of this Lot contains as area of 139,885 superficial square yards.

It might be pointed out that the property is capable of being converted into one of the finest Race-courses in England, if laid out as such round the outer edge of the Estate.

The auction catalogue then goes on to list all the fixtures and buildings offered for sale within the Gardens. It at times is hard to believe that such a vast and complex entertainment, sporting and horticultural site was so readily broken up and disposed off.

The following is a list of the Fixtures included in Lot 1:

1. All the Electric Lighting, fittings, lamps and globes throughout the grounds. All gas fittings, lamps, and globes throughout the grounds. All electric light and gas fittings throughout the buildings (save and except the Cut Glass Gasalier in the Auditorium of Indian Village or Pavilion, and a Bronze Chandelier in the Grand Opera House, and several spare Electric Lamps in Engine House which are in the valuation of loose effects.

2. All the Figures mounted on Pedestals throughout the Gardens as fixed.

3. Iron Pagoda Summer House in the grounds, with 4 fixed seats.

4. All Fountains and their Attachments in the grounds as fixed.

5. Seal Pond, Figures, Fountains, and Rock Work as fixed.

6. All Firework Fixings forming the Cascade Falls, together with all Wire Ropes and Winch, in Italian Gardens.

7. All Firework Patterns, Models, and Designs in wood and iron.

8. The outside Dancing Stage as laid.

9. All troughs for Fairy Fountain.

10. The whole of the Niagara Building Picture and Panoramic Scene of Niagara.

11. Large outside Pagoda Design Aviary.

12. The Rockery and Well in Monkey House as planted.

13. All caging for animals and birds in Monkey House, and Mechanical Appliances for Monkey gymnasts, the Heating Apparatus, all Staging and Tables for models, all Gas Fittings in Monkey House.

14. In Indian Lounge & Pavilion: All Canvas Painting as fixed around room, all Shelving and Counters, all the Partition forming Auditorium, Checker's Office, Partition and Gateway leading to Grand Stand from Lounge, the Partition forming orchestra, all Stage Machinery, Flies, and Counter in Bar, and Fixed Mirrors at the back of bar, Shelving, all the Stalls in Bazaar (except those owned by tenants).

15. In Ballroom: Four Bars, Counters, and all Fixed Mirrors and Shelving behind first-class bars, all the Mirrors in the Pillars about the Ballroom, all Lavatory Basins and Fast Fixtures in Lavatories and Cloak-room, with 418 Receptacles for Cloaks, Coats, and Sticks, all Stalls.

16. In Billiard Room: All Electric Light and Gas Light Fittings (except the Billiard Chandeliers), all Bar Counters, with Shelving and Fixed Mirrors behind.

17. The old Ballroom and lean-to Stall outside (contents belong to tenant).

18. The Photographic Studio at the east end of the Engine Room.

19. The Electric Lighting Plant includes a New Compound Engine (Horizontal) by Burnley Iron Company, two New Dynamos (made by Newton & Taunton), each driven by four ropes, new Switch Board, three Amperes or Ammetres, a 'Globe' Engine running two Dynamos of Pattison & Company type, driven by two six inch leather belts, Bailey's Feed Pump for Boiler, large Double-Acting Pump (by Goodbrand of Manchester) for pumping water to the Fairy Fountain.

20. A 'Lion' Safety Valve – High Pressure Steam Valve with Steam Gauge.

21. E.P.S., L. Type Cells as fixed [some kind of battery storage cells].

22. The Engine House, Boiler Hosue, Workshops, Joiners' Shops, Cabinet Maker and Blacksmith Shops, with Fixture Bench 15 feet long.

23. All Propagating Houses.

24. All Loose Lights for Forcing Frames [Bedding plant propagators].

25. In Grand Opera House: all Machinery and Drop Scene, Flies on Stage, all fast Seating in Gallery, all Fast Fixtures and Seating, Bar Counter, Bar Fittings, Cupboards as fixed with Shelves over same in Vaults.

26. Enamelled Curb Fender and Tiled Heart in Smoke Room.

27. In Anti-Room behind: All fixed Shelving Partitions forming back of office; a Hoist Frame; all Fixed Counters and Shelving.

28. Shelving in Bottom Office.

29. Gardener's Cottage – two pay offices.

30. All fixed Tables and Shelves in Kitchens, Hoe Water Cylinder, Wash-up Trough, with H. & C. Taps.

31. In Grand Café Bar: Mahogany Top Counter with recesses behind; all Shelving and Fixed Mirrors behind, Fixed Glazed Cigar Cupboard, Glass Keg recesses, with Mirror Backs, and a fixed Mirror at each end of bar.

32. In Stores under Theatre and Bottling Department; Fixed Counter and Shelves on the left of entrance, Wine Bins enclosed with sliding Cupboards, office as fixed with Letter Rack, Shelves and Book Rack, Counter and Iron Safe thereon. A 19 feet Counter with Shelving over, a Fixture Range of Sliding Cupboards.

33. In Spirit Cellar: all Shelving, Staging, on east side, short length on south side, and shelving on south side left of doorway.

34. Bottling Wash Vat with patent filler, Washing Tubs &c.

Lot 2:

All That PLOT OF LAND situate on the southerly side of Lot 1, containing in the whole 13,154 square yards, together with the brick built erections standing thereon, now used as a firework manufactory, and being fully licensed as such. A portion of this Lot is enclosed with timber fencing over 6ft. high. The site is a suitable one for [house] building purposes, and forms as at present used a very necessary adjunct to the Company's Business.

Lot 3:

All that PLOT OF LAND situate at the corner of Raikes Parade, Hornby Road, and Park Road, Blackpool, containing 3,077 square yards or thereabouts. This is very eligible Building Plot, having extensive frontages to three of the most desirable streets in the town for the erection of high-class Residences.

Some of the smaller and surplus plots of land were sold off but the main Gardens area in Lot 1 was not sold and failed to attract the right price. Therefore it continued on for another couple of years. It would have its final flourish before the inevitable happened. In a way the Gardens went out with a bang and defied the odds so firmly stacked against it.

BLACKPOOL, Lancashire.

PLANS AND PARTICULARS

OF THE

ROYAL PALACE GARDENS

THE PROPERTY OF

RAIKES HALL

Park, Gardens, Aquarium Co., Ltd.,

WITH THE

FULLY LICENSED HOTEL,

And Other Buildings thereon, situate at

BLACKPOOL,

TO BE

SOLD BY AUCTION,

BY

MESSRS. T. CARTER & CO.,

IN THE

GRAND OPERA HOUSE, within the Grounds,

ON

MONDAY, the 13th day of July, 1896,

AT FOUR O'CLOCK IN THE AFTERNOON.

FINCH & JOHNSON,
SOLICITORS,
BLACKPOOL AND PRESTON.

H. MAXWELL & Co., Printers, 74, Church Street, Blackpool.

The cover of the Auction Catalogue for the Royal Palace Gardens in 1896

Royal Palace Gardens

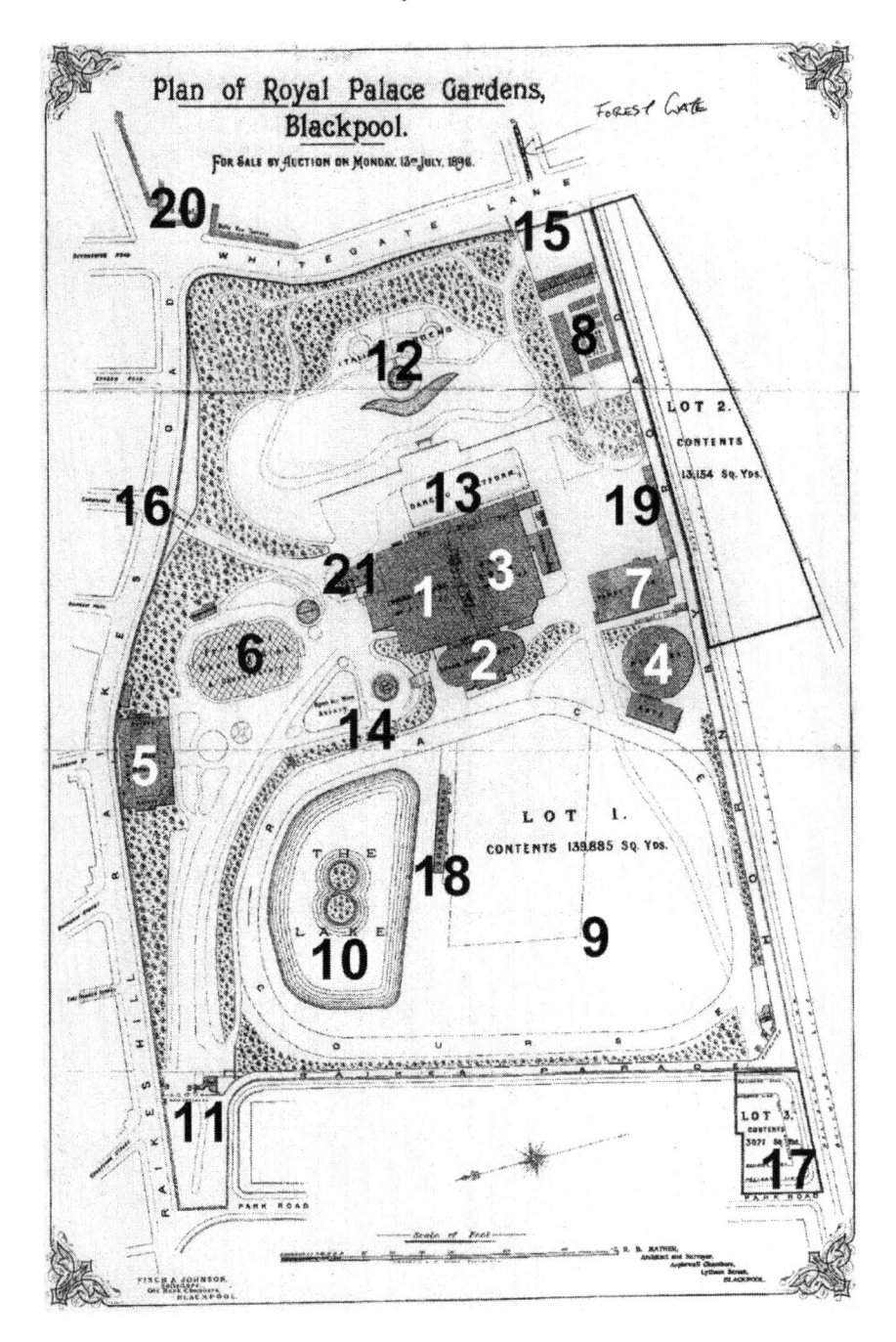

Plan of Royal Palace Gardens, Blackpool.

For Sale by Auction on Monday, 13th July, 1896.

Royal Palace Gardens

Map number reference is as follows:

1. Indian Village / Theatre & Pavillion with Billiard Rooms and Bars
2. Grand Opera House & Bars
3. Ballroom & Bars
4. Niagara Exhibition & Cafe
5. Aviary & Monkey House
6. Grand Conservatory, Ferneries & Skating Rink
7. Blacksmiths Workshops, Stables and Workshops
8. Vineries & Greenhouses
9. Sports Field & Race Track
10. Boating Lake & Island
11. Main Entrance at junction with Church Street and Park Road
12. Italian Gardens & Fairy Fountain
13. Open Air Dancing Platform
14. Open air Wire Aviary & Seal Pond
15. Entrance from Whitegate Lane (now Drive) at Hornby Road junction.
16. Entrance from Raikes Road (now Church Street) opposite Cambridge Road.
17. Entrance from Hornby Road at Park Road junction.
18. Sports Field Grandstand, Changing Rooms and Bars.
19. Firework Factory
20. Site of the Number 3 (Didsbury Hotel) at Devonshire Square.
21. Raikes Hall Hotel (only building that still exists in 2016).

The Gardens were designed to be viewed on foot or by horse and carriage via its many drives and vistas. The area that is outlined as Plot 2 on the right is on the south side of Hornby Road at the Whitegate Drive end. This is mostly houses with the old Bank on the corner next to Michael Bridges shop and the Guards Club.

Raikes Hill and Raikes Road (on left of the map) have now been renamed and become a continuation of Church Street to Devonshire Square.

Chapter 12

THE FINAL CURTAIN

By 1897 Queen Victoria's reign had lasted 60 years. Most British town of consequence celebrated the occasion in grand style. Blackpool was no exception. All the resorts major entertainment venues were brightly decorated for the occasion of the Diamond Jubilee. As a mark of patriotic respect the Royal Palace Gardens managing director Charles Iddeson introduced many celebratory dances and fetes throughout the season.

One of the popular public relations exercises was aimed at helping the town's under privileged and older residents who were wined and dined at the expense of the directors. In fact during the height of the 1897 summer, the entrance fee was waived for a week. As a result thousands flocked to the Gardens. The main attraction was the serving of fine ale and food. On a good day as many as 2,000 set meals were served, enthusiastically prepared by a catering staff headed by Mr. Mrs. William Bamber. During 1897 Charles Iddeson, forever the sporting promoter, continued to organize his beloved horse trotting meetings although, arguably, his major sporting interest was athletics in the form of professional foot racing.

Athletic events in their amateur form had been held at the Gardens since the early 1870s. The runners originally competed on a simple grass track, yet through the years the directors had gradually upgraded the track, and added the fine grandstand. Many local amateur runners took full advantage of the Gardens facilities and in 1894 the Blackpool Harriers held their first athletics festival there. Iddeson's idea was to create a series of Great Pedestrian Races. Most of the races were to be short sprints of up to 130 yards in length. The sprints were determined under professional handicap rules, with prize money fixed at £100 per final – a considerable amount of money for the time. With such generous prize money, the Gardens was a definite winner too, becoming a sporting Mecca attracting hundreds of athletics followers. Colliers from Yorkshire, foundry men from the Black Country, cotton workers form Lancashire mills, all competed for the prize money.

Many of the top athletes of the day also competed including Charles Harper and Charley Bradley. Huddersfield's Bradley was a character and a half who won the Amateur Athletic Association's 100 yard race for four consecutive years, whose marvellous amateur days came to an end in July 1896 at London's Anderton Hotel. Here a special meeting of the AAA was convened, where Bradley and five other amateur athletes were banned from competing in amateur contests for life. Their crime was to receive forbidden cash payments – against amateur rules and the reason for their harsh punishment.

Charles Bradley [the Flying Tyke was his nickname] was to athletics what Mohammed Ali was to boxing. A highly talented, flamboyant character who was adored and revered by the public. He was a product of the 1890s – the golden years of British Athletics. He trained at the numerous tracks in Blackpool including that at the Royal Palace Gardens. In retrospect the Flying Tyke will always be remembered for his speed and talent, but above all for his Yorkshire grit and humour. The latter immortalised in the 1893 AAA 100 yard championship at Northampton when Charley, always looking for a sprint record, was told by officials that if he broke any records they would not be ratified because the track was slightly downhill with a following wind. Charley's reply, given in a strong Yorkshire dialect was: "Well then I'll oop t'hill and againth t'wind, then can say nowt!" He did, winning in a record breaking 10 seconds!

The future of the Royal Palace Gardens attracted interest from far and wide. Letters by the dozens arrived at the Blackpool's local paper. One concerned reader from Huddersfield, on hearing of the possible future as building land, thought it would be a much better idea to change it into a public park – run by the council. Even suggesting that as it had changed its name for Queen Victoria's Golden Jubilee it could be renamed Queens Park in honour of her Diamond Jubilee. He advised the wealthy and loyal citizens of Blackpool to help the council purchase it and turn it into Blackpool's equivalent of London's Kensington Gardens.

A sharp contrast to the patriotic Royal festivities of 1897 was the sad death in his London home, Niagara House, of Charles Blondin. The great French high wire artist was the toast of the Royal Palace Gardens some two years earlier in 1895, when thousands of visitors witnessed his death defying act.

At the end of 1897 and the early part of 1898, plans were in place for the forthcoming holiday season in spite of the company failing to sell the Gardens at auction the previous July. Money was tight and capital investment in the Gardens was virtually non existent, yet undeterred, Charles Iddeson, soldiered on. He booked, despite a limited budget, many talented variety artistes. They included the toast of the music halls – funny man Harry Rogerson – and the charming burlesque artist Flo Wood.

Throughout the 1898 season the Gardens still dominated the Blackpool public's interest. Seaside rumour was rife about an impending takeover by a syndicate of London entrepreneurs. During the August of 1898 this ambitious group put their plans for the Gardens before the Blackpool Council Building Plans Committee. One of the leading protagonists in the London group was the son of Earls Court architect Mr. Charles Imre Kilralfi. He proposed the complete removal or demolition of all the Gardens present attractions. The plans included for a new grand entrance located in the same area as the present principal entrance (where the Salvation Army Citadel now stands at Church Street). The patrons would pass through impressive gates into a magnificent and roomy entrance hall. Immediately to the right of the proposed new entrance gates was to be a huge theatre, the largest in the world, capable of seating some 8,000 persons. Gracing the stage would be historical or operatic ballets, naval, military and other spectacular productions. Adjoining the theatre would be a restaurant, and continuing along Raikes Parade to the corner of Hornby Road would be a representation of Venice with replica Bridge of Sighs, waterways, gondolas all leading to a secondary entrance.

On the south side of the Gardens, the proposed plans included a spectacular water chute and behind the new grand theatre was to be the site of a new open air dancing platform. Beyond a new north terrace would be a panorama with a stage adjoining. Near the east terrace was the proposed site of a new lake, with linked waterways spanned by many bridges and a fountain in the centre of the lake. Two prettily designed courts were proposed for each side of the lake, which would be surrounded on three sides by shops and arcades. In addition to this the plans proposed exhibition halls and side shows where fine art and industrial and manufacturing exhibitions would be held.

Sadly the radical plans for the Gardens came to nothing. Various excuses came out of the Blackpool Corporation Planning Department. One theory being that a number of the resorts leading entertainment impresarios formed an opposition group who collectively lobbied planners to throw out the southerners ambitious plans.

During 1898 rugby once again graced the Gardens sporting arena. This time it was played under amateur league rules – but alas after 17 matches and an equal amount of losses the Blackpool Rugby Club folded in 1899. The demise of rugby was ironically at the same time as the retirement of the Royal Palace Gardens sporting and entertainment visionary, Charles Iddeson. Iddeson had guided the Gardens complex through good times and indifferent times. His resignation from the management board created just the opening that another longtime employee, William Bamber, had patiently waited for. He was offered the role as manager and eagerly accepted. He would be the last.

At the opening of the 1899 season the Gardens horticultural displays were in their usual resplendent order, yet there were signs of general neglect within the grounds. Many of the buildings were showing signs of deterioration and neglect. The Easter festivities opened with a flourish. Football being the main attraction, three of the visiting teams were Darwen, Leicester Fosse and Newton Heath.

One of the most popular of Victorian pursuits was the equine sport of trotting, and through the years the Gardens arena had played an important role, so much so that by 1899 the venue was second only in importance to the north's leading centre, Manchester. At a September 1889 meeting the famous trotting mare Polly G. driven by Metcalfe created trotting history by breaking the world 4 mile record when she circled the Garden's track in 9 minutes and 58 seconds, some 9 seconds faster than the existing record. During the same month the Royal Institute For Public Health held their annual conference at the Royal Palace Gardens.

On the international front the outbreak of the Boer War captured the 1899 headlines. The conflict, although on some foreign field, had far reaching consequences. The British public broke out in a military fever and patriotism was high. Many national and local trades people hooked on the events in the "toe of Africa". The Boer War rekindled the thoughts of many locals who maintained that the Gardens should become a public park incorporating a grand shooting range. Blackpool of course had been a base for troops for many years, where hundreds, if not thousands, of soldiers had made their summer camp on land adjacent to Whitegate Lane (now Whitegate Drive).

One of the most memorable events of the Boer War was the siege of Mafeking, where heroic British troops were commanded by Baden Powell. It is the same Baden Powell who visited the Gardens in July of 1887. The occasion was a grand military tournament held on the sports field. Powell, then a young captain in the 13th Hussars, took part.

Savage South Africa

It was the sensation of late Victorian entertainment, regarded by many as the show of the century. It's title was 'Savage South Africa', and it appeared as an attraction in Blackpool. After a record breaking success at London's Earls Court, and at the Broughton Rangers Football Ground, Salford. It's arrival in late July 1900 at Talbot Railway Station (North Station) was witnessed by hundreds of bystanders. Three special trains were needed to convey the show's menagerie and entertainers. Outside the station, the company quickly formed themselves into a professional procession in order to march to their destination at the Royal Palace Gardens. A Dutch Afrikaaner band led the way, playing the stirring music of Soldiers of the Queen and the Bay of Biscay. Following the musicians were the Elephants, Lions, Horses, Mules, Ponies, Oxen, Wilderbeest and Baboons – some 150 animals in all. Behind the animals marched the keepers, rough riders, Boers and Afrikaaners, Yankees, Australians, Colonials, Zulus, Basutos and Matabeles. Men in khaki marched four deep, their rifles slung across their shoulders. The Jack Tars and British Troopers trundled their Maxim Guns behind them. The black folk rode in waggonettes, most attired in English dress – although many were in ceremonial war paint as well!

Most of the entertainers soon settled in Blackpool, and all day the Zulus, Matabele and Basutos could be seen parading the resort's streets and promenades. The show's managing director was Mr. J. Pitt Hardacre, and the manager's role was taken by Mr. G. H. Brooke's. However, the driving force behind the show's popularity was the originator and inventor of the show was a London born 43 year old named Frank E. Fillis. The showman supreme came from a family of performers and adventurers, notably his father and his uncle James who also had a love for animals – that Frank also shared. Uncle James, notably, was the equine-in-chief to the Tsar of Russia no less, and was recognized as one of the greatest professors of horsemanship in the world.

Frank Fillis had all the attributes of his famous uncle. Upon travelling to South Africa in 1887 he became one of the first on the Transvaal Goldfields. Here he purchased some property cheaply, which subsequently increased in value considerably and proved to be a shrewd investment. With the profits he gathered together a collection of rare wild animals and started a small circus type show, which eventually grew into the sensational Savage South Africa extravaganza!

During his two decades on the continent of Africa, Fillis became friends with many notables including President Kruger, President Steyri, Generals Joubert, Louis Botha, De Wet, Cronje and Baden Powell. Fillis was described as the African Barnum, yet he always maintained his shows were different – describing the Barnum and Bailey Circus as a show that seeks to amuse, whereas Savage South Africa seeks to amuse, but also tries to educate. It was enthusiastically billed as The Greatest Show On Earth! And it lived up to its hype.

Perfect weather and a tremendous publicity campaign attracted one of the largest crowds for almost a decade. It was the 23rd July 1900 and the opening of the sensational Savage South Africa. The show was centred on the Gardens football ground, but actually occupied all the Gardens open spaces. The exhibitions setting was that of an amphitheatre, with the arena in the centre representing the African veldt. On three sides of the arena at a cost of 3 shillings, 2 shillings and 1 shilling, were seats for 2,000 spectators. The western end of the arena was left open, here there was a realistic scene depicting a mountain range and river – the authentic looking rocks actually made from papier-mâché – most of the south east corner of the Garden's trotting track was occupied by a large Kaffir – Krall (Native Village). One of the Krall residents was a magnificent specimen of manhood and what is more, he was an African Royal as well. He was the third son of the old Matabele King Lobengula and his tenth wife, with his official title being Prince Peter Lobengula. His well furnished hut had a touch of patriotic allegiance, with pictures of Queen Victoria and the British Royal family adorning his walls.

Nestling around Prince Lobengula's hut were also the temporary homes of many African Chiefs including: Manoedi, Omleonmlie, Omleongeu, Gebruzla, Messeau, Siomeza, and Diza a Zulu chief. Diza was interviewed by the local Gazette journalist, who was surprised at the Zulu's command of the English language. Diza had actually been educated at one of the Cape colonies leading colleges.

For a general entrance fee of a Tanner (that's 6d in old money – equivalent to 2 & half new pennies today) the patrons could wander through the native village and the elephant tents. Many of the native women earned an extra few coppers from the sale of their decorative beads and trinkets.

Another novelty on sale throughout the Gardens was the forerunner of today's lettered sticks of rock, but it was sticks of butter scotch with the name Baden Powell at one end and Lord Kitchener at the other.

Across from the native Kralls camp was the Boer's encampment. Pier Visser was a Boer soldier, or Laager, and stood at a staggering 6 feet 8 inches tall. Visser was the son of the Chief Detective of the Transvaal. The show that he participated in featured a marvellous reenactment of colonial life with scenes illustrating Boer's at peace and war. There were many exhibitions of riding and driving by Africaaner ladies, Malays, Cape Boys,

Hottentots, Boer's, and the wonderful riding ponies, without saddle or stirrup, by the dare-devil Basutos. The troupe of elephants produced a spectacle never seen in Blackpool before. The elephant encampment is attacked by the Boer's during a show reconstruction, and during the ensuing conflict the commander is killed. The smallest elephant then limped forward and waved a white flag of surrender. Two giant tusked elephants then cover him with a Union Jack flag, lift him up and carry him away – all to the cheering delight of the Garden's thrilled audience.

Frank Fillis and his Spanish born wife Madame Fillis gave a wonderful display of Spanish High School Riding (Madame Fillis was recognized as the greatest lady horse rider in the world). Among the show's many performers was an Irish Boer, James Keighry, who for many years was the sate coachman to President Kruger. He was also the driver of the Gwela Coach, when it was attacked by the Matables with alarming consequences in 1896. The whole sequence of events were re-enacted in the show.

Another larger than life character who played an adventurous role in the show was Andries Ventnor who was with Kronjies forces at the capture of the Jameson Raiders. He represented the last stand of Major Allan Wilson and his 34 gallant men on the banks of the Shanghai River. When the men stood shoulder to shoulder and sang the National Anthem the spectators gave a round of applause. The re-creation of the Battle of Elandslaahgte was excitement taken to the extreme, with several maxin guns brought into the show. During the proceedings a trooper and his horse leap over a precipice in to the water some 30 feet below.

The hunting of animals was also depicted, and the imaginations of the observers must have ran wild when a lion was let loose and crossed the mountain range (although it was not as it seemed, the lion ingeniously fastened by a harness and a strong chain). The show's finale came when in rode the magnificent figure of the noted scout, Texas Jack, leading a procession of the show's artistes. The music throughout the spectacle was played by the Afrikaaner Band under the direction of Signor Capra. Quite a show at quite a price! Production costs were in the region of £1,800 per week. But was Savage South Africa ultimately The Greatest Show On Earth?

From all accounts Savage South Africa was a financial disaster. Thousands of guests had flocked to see the amazing show – much to the delight of the Garden's managers. The general delight had been overshadowed by several mishaps. During August a spate of freak weather likened to a monsoon completely flattened the troopers encampment, and the elephant tent.

During the exciting re-enactment of the Battle of Elandslaaghte a horse suffered a serious injury and had to be destroyed by Frank Fillis. Expert rough rider William Eldred had a heavy fall and broke his leg. The to top it all, there was the dilemma of many of the show's authentic performers, most of which were originally engaged by Fillis in South Africa, returning to their homeland as a result of the hostilities and another war.

To keep the show running Fillis scoured the country for replacements, taking on a motley crew of Malays, Jamaicans, Indians and even an English based South American Indian. Savage South Africa's reign at the Royal Palace Gardens ended on 15th September 1900 with its final days beset with a number of ugly incidents. Numerous scuffles and fights had broken out at the resort's taverns and nearby public houses between the Boer's and Zulus – aided by a handful of locals eager to create trouble. Animosity reached a crescendo one balmy summer evening in late August 1900. A fight that took on the ugly characteristics of a racial riot began when several Kaffirs were winding their way back to the Gardens. Some remarks were made by a group of bystanders as they passed near the main entrance gates at Raikes Parade. Within minutes dozens of the natives swarmed out of their Kraals like angry bees. Opposing them were many of the trouble making locals. Thankfully the show supreme Frank Fillis was alerted by staff at the Gardens, allowing him to intervene and save a full scale fight – that would have had far reaching and more serious consequences.

During the same month of August the Gardens future once more captured the public's attention. An open meeting was held at the Albion Hotel, where local auctioneer Carter & Sons offered for sale the Raikes Hall Estate and Royal Palace Gardens. Alderman Bickerstaff and Charles Iddeson were amongst the notable public figures who attended. Iddeson spoke on the merits of the Raikes and the Gardens and stated that Savage South Africa had the potential to attract thousands of visitors – as many as 30,000 per day. Although this seems to be highly exaggerated if not desperately optimistic. He then went on to highlight the fact that Blackpool, a town of 50,000 residents, had no museum, art gallery, reference library, public baths, recreation ground or public park. He stated that the £80,000 needed to purchase the Gardens was well within the means of Blackpool Council. His point it seems is that the Gardens had the potential to provide some of the amenities mentioned and persuading the council to purchase would secure the Gardens future.

The auctioneer offered the whole estate, some 22 acres in a couple of lots at a knock down price of £72,000 but no offers were received. Some small plots for building were sold. Rumours persisted throughout the summer as to the fate of the Gardens but it seemed that everything was in vain and that, in spite of the relative success of Savage South Africa, that the end of the road was in sight for the Raikes Hall and the Royal Palace Gardens.

During the early part of May 1901, the Raikes Directors announced, with great optimism, that a London based American Showman, John Cameron McLaughlin had leased the Gardens from the beginning of May 1901. His intention was to organize a World Fair incorporating two spectacular shows The Siege & Relief of Mafeking, and The Scalp Hunters. Early arrangements for the season began in earnest, when workmen by the score descended on the Gardens to erect the side-shows, scenery, and huge grandstand. Their was much excitement when the spectacular shows eventually opened on 15th July 1901. Enthusiastic audiences, along with fantastic weather, encouraged an excited first day crowd. The show's first days, especially the stirring military scenes at Mafeking were, as advertised and promised, exciting indeed. The performances of American high wire artist, Hardy, revived memories of the great Blondin. Leoni Clarke's animals, and Landerman's Boxing Kangeroos created much interest.

Yet within a week events took on a different tone. The saga came to a head at the end of the first week, when the entertainers and workmen queued up to be paid. Even though the first week's taking were, seemingly anyway, reasonable there was insufficient money to pay anyone their wages. Averting a riot with promises of payment, an embarrassed McLaughlin left for London for more money.

The rumours were rife in Blackpool about the state of the London company's finances. As a consequence many of the show's stall holders removed themselves and their property from the Gardens. In addition, a local furnishing company removed hundreds of chairs from the Indian Theatre Lounge because they had not been paid. Even a 41 foot balloon used in the Gardens by the soap company Hudsons for advertising purposes was quickly dismantled and removed.

History of Raikes Hall

RAIKES HALL
BLACKPOOL.

INSTANTANEOUS SUCCESS!!

OPEN FOR THE SEASON
IN THE OPEN AIR.

GREATEST ATTRACTIONS
EVER SEEN IN BLACKPOOL.

THE GRAND MILITARY SPECTACLE
THE SIEGE & RELIEF OF MAFEKING.

Produced by PAIN & SONS, of London & New York
Pronounced by Press and Public to be the Most
Successful Show ever seen in Blackpool.

GIGANTIC DISPLAY OF FIREWORKS.

"THE SCALP HUNTERS,"
TWICE DAILY, introducing the Celebrated
DIVING HORSES.
Produced by JOHN HENRY COOKE
(Cook's Royal Circus).

In the Open Air, Twice Daily,
HARDY,
The Greatest Mid-Air Performance in the World.
HEATON,
Terrific High Dive.
PONGO on the Rope.
ALVANTE,
The King of the Slanting Wire.
&c., &c., &c.

The Celebrated Trotting Mare,
"LADY R."
Twice Daily.

'THE CARNIVAL,
Direct from the Crystal Palace, London.
TWICE DAILY in the IMPERIAL THEATRE.

LEONI CLARKE,
The Cat King.
At 3-0 p.m., 4-0 p.m., 6-0 p.m., and 9-45 p.m., in the
IMPERIAL THEATRE, with his marvellous CATS,
RATS, CANARIES, MONKEYS, RABBITS, &c., &c.

THE BOXING KANGAROO,
Introduced by
DICK LANDERMAN.
TWICE DAILY in the MONKEY HOUSE.

DANCING ALL DAY

ABSOLUTELY THE FINEST
PERFORMANCES
EVER SEEN IN BLACKPOOL.

(ALL DAY)
6D.—ADMISSION—6D.

1901

The Last Show! The Siege & Relief of Mafeking – still only 6d admission.

The show was finished and many of the contractors who had worked so hard on constructing the show went bust. The site labourers had insufficient money to pay for their living expenses and digs and ended up camping out in the Gardens, with many taking refuge in the old Monkey House – now empty and awaiting demolition. For over a week the disgruntled workers had to depend on hastily organized soup kitchens. Eventually the police had to evict them from the Gardens. The infamous impresario, McLaughlin, never returned to Blackpool with the promised money. The truth eventually came out. A year later McLaughlin appeared before a bankruptcy court to explain his financial standing and role in the sorry affair. He explained how he borrowed a thousand pounds to float the project at the Royal Palace Gardens. The debts stood at nearly £10,000. Money he could never repay.

End of an Era!

The sad loss of the summer show at the Gardens was the final nail in the coffin, one the directors could have done without. Enthusiasm was at an all time low. In fact, for the first time in almost thirty years, there was no money spent advertising for the traditional August Bank Holiday. Minor functions were still held in the main Raikes Hotel in the Gardens. Trotting meetings were still held but revenue was insufficient to meet overheads.

Many of the major buildings, including the main theatre, were in need of maintenance, and many others were in a dilapidated state. Small parcels of building land had been sold of during the previous two years, yet there were still major tracts of land for sale. The Gardens were diminished and past their best.

Once again the directors put the remaining land up for sale, the area included the Niagara Cafe site of some 3,333 square yards, and the Raikes plot that included the original hall, Indian Lounge, Theatre and Ballroom. This land was eventually sold for 12 shillings per square yard.

Bit by bit, by November 1901, most of the Royal Palace Gardens, a Victorian entertainment wonderland to rival the Tivoli Gardens, had been sold for mainly building houses. One of the last events of note was the draining of the Gardens boating lake. Eerily the lake, once a fishing and boating paradise, had no fish left except for one two foot long eel!

At the end of November 1901, the road makers and house builders were in charge. Their efforts produced what we see today in the area that the Royal Palace Gardens once occupied. All that remains is the original hall, now the

Raikes Public House. The decline of the Gardens is hard to fathom, especially as John Bickerstaff had a hand in its management in the years prior to its demise. Was it deliberately allowed to fail? Why was it not bought by the town? There is no doubt it was seen a direct threat to the Tower, Winter Gardens and the Piers. Perhaps the powers that be in the town decided that they wanted to concentrate the holiday crowds on the coastal areas and didn't want them going inland. Maybe we shall never know the true reason.

However, had the Royal Palace Gardens survived they would undoubtedly be a world heritage site today. Blackpool's lost Victorian pleasure Gardens would have stood shoulder to shoulder with the Tivoli Gardens and been an enormous heritage attraction for the town and its economy. Like so many things in Blackpool, the opportunity was also lost. But at least we have the history and the wonderful stories of how the Royal Palace Gardens helped put Blackpool on the map as a tourist resort long before the Tower, Winter Gardens, Opera House or piers were built and ultimately sealed its fate by their dominance. Thankfully the Raikes Hall stands proud, a fine Georgian manor hall still, trading today as a public house surrounded by houses. What fantastic history is part of all their foundations. It is all we have left of the fabulous Royal Palace Gardens.

The Raikes Hall – the land in the foreground sold and ready to be built on. The extension to the right of the building was added in Circa. 1894. The Gardens now demolished. Circa 1902.

Raikes Hall as it stands today, surrounded by residential streets that have been built on the grounds of the Royal Palace Gardens.

For more information on the Raikes Hall please see their website for details:

http://www.raikeshallblackpool.co.uk

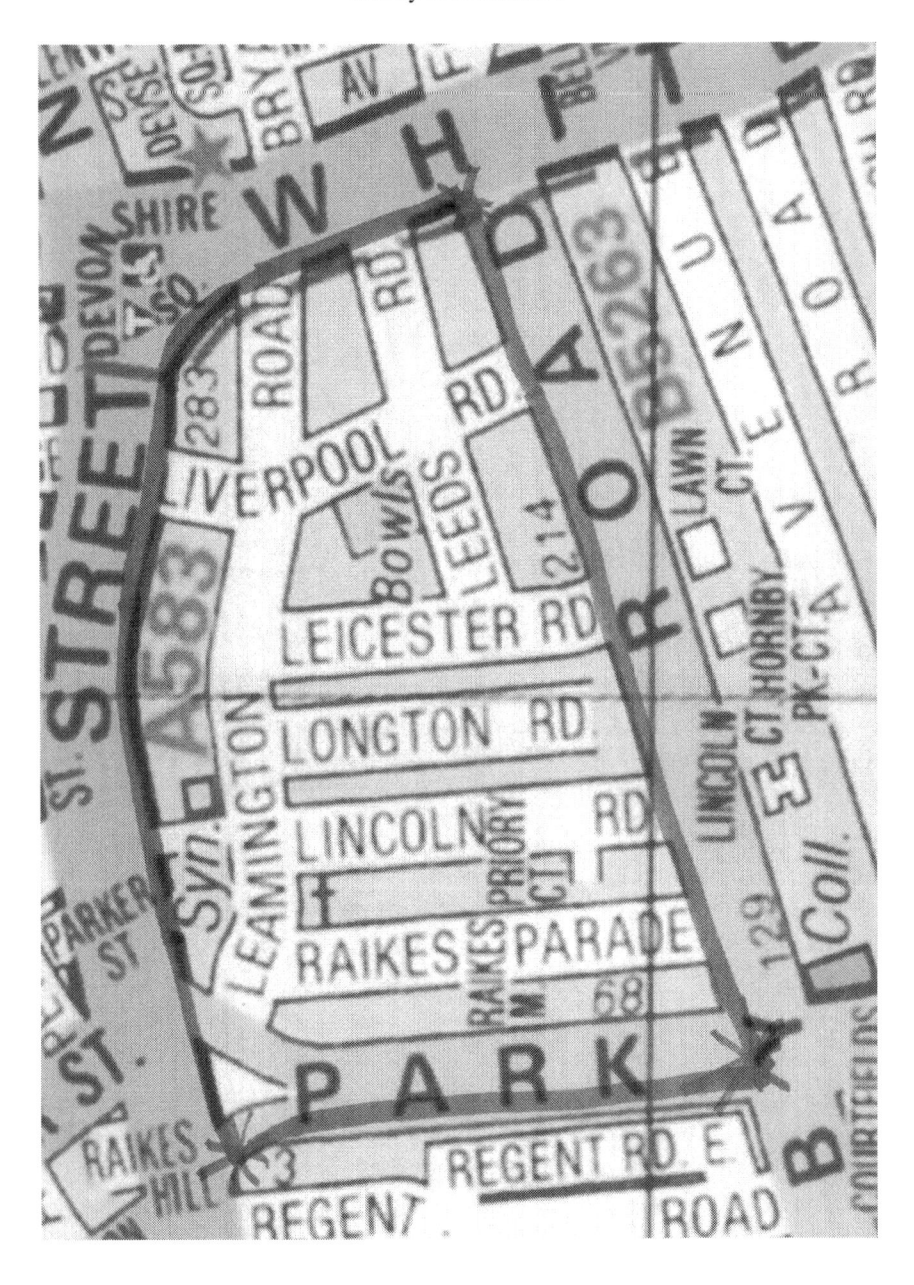

The area in green shows the outline of where the Royal Palace Gardens was situated.

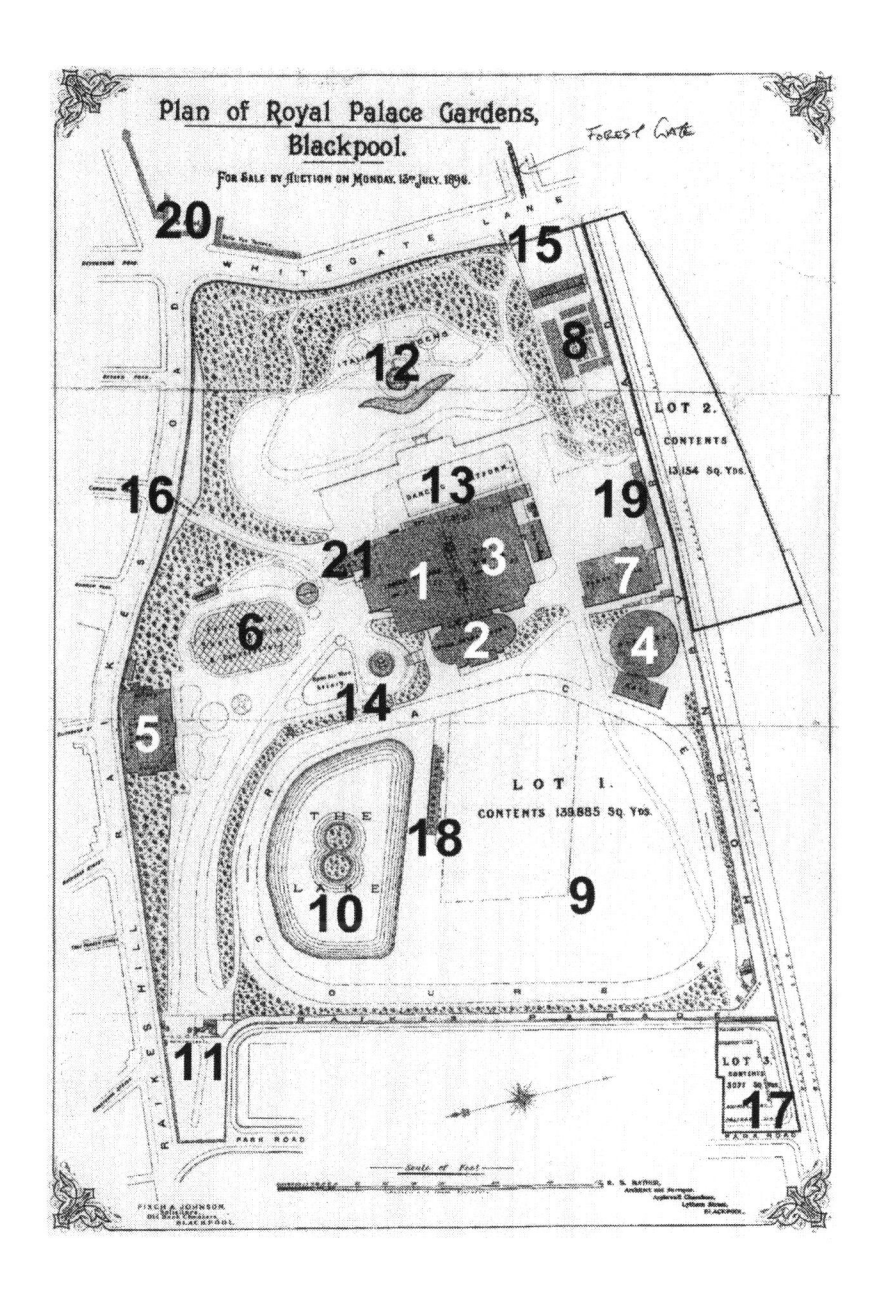

Plan of Royal Palace Gardens, Blackpool.
FOR SALE BY AUCTION ON MONDAY, 13th JULY, 1896.

FOREST GATE

Many artistes of the late Victorian period performed at the Royal Palace Gardens. This programme from the Tivoli Theatre, Strand, London 1895 which includes the popular Jenny Valmore (The Lavender Girl) – who was a favourite of the Royal Palace Gardens. So many have slipped into obscurity with so little know about them. Sad as that is, many have been indentified for this book and where possible biographies created in the Reference section of this book.

Thanks to Matthew at Arthur Lloyd's History for this image - More information about this fantastic resource at

www.arthurlloyd.co.uk

References

Further Reading:

Eyre, Kathleen. **Seven Golden Miles**. Dalesman Publishing, Lancaster, 1961.

Flaxman, Radegunde. **A Woman Styled Bold – The Life of Cornelia Connelly**. Dartman, Longman & Todd Publishers Ltd, London, 1991.

Mother Therese, Maria. **Cornelia Connelly – A Study in Fidelity**. Burns & Oats Publishers, London, 1961.

Assael, Brenda. **The Circus & Victorian Society**. University of Virginia Press, USA, 2005.

Scott, Derek, B. **Sounds of the Metropolis – The 19th Century Popular Music Revolution**. Oxford University Press, Oxford, 2011.

Gillet, Paula. **Musical Women in England 1870-1914** – Encroaching on all Mans Privelidges. Palgrave Macmillan Publishers, 2000.

Baker, Richard Anthony. **British Music Hall – An Illustrated History**. Sutton Publishing Ltd, Gloucestershire, 2005.

St Mary' Academy History. Society of the Holy Child Jesus. **Issue II: The Significance of Place**

Walton, John K.. **Leisure In Britain, 1780-1939**. Manchester University Press, 1986.

Myers American Circus – more information on the history of this circus availaable at Circiopedia's website:

www.circopedia.org/Myers'_Great_American_Circus

Hengler's Circus – more information on this circus available at this website:

www.theglasgowstory.com/image/?inum=TGSA00290

Savage South Africa touring show –

"One of the earliest films depicting African situations, the self-descriptive Savage South Africa. The show [the film is taken from] is a dramatic reenactment of a real-life event from the Metabele wars between African natives and British infantry. It was filmed in London – the African performers genuine enough. They were originally brought over [to the United Kingdom] by the South African impresario Frank Fillis, whose spectacular Earls Court how Savage South Africa [then brought to the Royal Palace Gardens at Raikes Hall] blended stage performances and exhibitions where visitors could wander among semi-naked Africans.

This latter aspect was particularly popular with women, though the essential hypocrisy of Victorian society at the time was exposed when the show's star, Peter Lobengula (who claimed to be the son of the Matable King Lobengula) fell in love with an English girl, Kitty Jewell. Predictably, this led to a huge scandal, the flames of which were heavily fanned by the English popular press."

Michael Brooke - Entry in the BFI Catalogue. If nothing else this rare film preserves the performances of Savage South Africa that would have thrilled audiences at the Royal Palace Gardens. More information via this website:

www.screenonline.org.uk/film/id/725486

Whilst researching this book I have been able to identify in excess of 50 variety and music hall artistes who appeared at the Gardens from 1872 until the closure in 1901. Thanks to the Music Hall Guild of Great Britain, especially Matthew and Adrian, I have been able to compile some short biographies for some of those artistes. For others there was just no information available, artistes did use stage names – and still do – so the task made more difficult because of that - but I have listed their names anyway to preserve them for posterity and give them a place in this history of that remarkable entertainment venue and the late Victorian period in which they performed.

David SC

Artistes who have been identified as appearing at the Gardens between 1872 and 1901:

1. Son Of The Desert (African Blondin)
2. Mr. Barr's Famous Flying Hawks
3. Gosling & Wright (Skaters & Dancers)
4. Saville Swallow Orchestra
5. Jean Santley & Mademoiselle Lilian (Grotesque Duettists & Burlesque)
6. Miss Carrie & Mr. Charles Moore (Bicyclists & Skaters)
7. Leotard Bosco (Raconteur)
8. Captain J.A. Whelan (Aeronaut/Balloonist)
9. Rastus The Flying Man (Ballooning/High Wire)
10. Monsieur Albin (Monster Cyclist/Iron Horse)
11. Herr John Holtum (King OF The Cannon)
12. Rose Myers Celebrated Horse Troupe
13. Little Valdo & Tom Felix (Clowns)
14. Alivante (King OF The Loose Wire)
15. John Cooper (Lion Tamer)
16. Frank Gillfort (High Wire)
17. Sisters Zagaro (Wondrous Lady Acrobats)
18. Miss Bertie Stokes (Ballads)
19. Latvo Sisters (Duettists & Dancers)
20. Miss Maggie Hunt (Ballads)

21. Zoro (Equibrilist)
22. White Minstrel Singers
23. Fernandez (Gymnastic Trio)
24. Professor Codman (Punch & Judy)
25. Bikee Taylor's Comic Opera Company
26. Glennies Marionettes
27. Lilo, Elspa & Echo (Flying Trapeze Troup)
28. Mr. C.D. Vere (Magician)
29. Miss Katie Laurence – The Original Daisy Bell (Serio Comic & Vocalist)
30. Miss Marie De Simecourt (Ballads)
31. Mrs Hunt's Ladies Orchestra
32. Leglere Acrobatic Troup
33. The Gerittis (Musical Clowns)
34. The Denamoes (Marvelous High Wire Acrobats)
35. Mr. Johny Whiteman (Comic)
36. Miss Conway (Mimic)
37. The Montanas (Illusionists/Magic)
38. Jenny Valmore (The People's Idol)
39. Gus Ellen (Prince of Comedians)
40. John Holturn
41. Captain Fowler (King OF The Rifle)
42. Miss Nellie Frazell (Champion Shot Of The World)
43. Blondin (High Wire Artist)
44. Professor Morritt's Flying Lady
45. Miss Nellie Stratton (Comic & Dancer)
46. Mark Sheridan (Comedian)
47. Miss Holtum (Lady Juggler)
48. Lottie Lennox (The Lavender Girl)
49. Gracie Lloyd (Singer/Comic & sister of Marie)
50. Harry Rogerson (Comedian)
51. Flo Wood (Burlesque Artist)
52. Charlie Harvey (Comedian)
53. Little Daisy Palmer (Ballads)
54. Rose Harvey (Ballads)
55. Charles Cassie (Comic)
56. Nora Gordon (Actress)
57. Edgar Granville (Comedian)

Circus and Travelling Shows:

1. Myers American Circus info @ http://www.circopedia.org/Main_Page
2. Charles Henglers Circus
3. Allen's Circus
4. Savage South Africa
5. The Siege & Relief of Mafeking
6.

Others – Non Performing:

1. Thomas Grieve & Sons (Outdoor Scenic Diorama Painters)
2. Messrs Firth & Sons (Scenic Designers/Painters) Manc. & London
3. Mr. Turner (Local Blackpool Fine Artist)
4. Captain Loxton Rawbone (Landscape Scenic Artist/ Niagara)
5. Phillip Poteaux (French Artist / Niagara Building

Artist Biographies:

Alphonsine La Belle Rose – Spiral Queen (1855 – 1947)

[Augusta Caroline Rosalie Wingfield] "One-time queen of the spiral, and one of the most spectacular figures in the variety [theatre] of the [1880s], planned her funeral 20 years ago to the last detail. On Wednesday she was buried at Blackpool Cemetary in a vault she then purchased.

Her act was sensational. Standing on a ball, two feet in circumferance, she manouvered it to the top of a forty foot spiral – span of ths spiral was 10 inches – she then came down backwards. She was paid £200 per week. A huge sum in those days.

When asked why she planned her funeral, she would say: 'I have lived like a Queen. I will die like one.'

She was buried, according to those long-ago instructions in a white coffin, dressed in the white silk she wore on the spiral with her beloved jewelled chain, ivory cross and ear-rings.

The vault was lined with white chrysanthemums, the entrance banked with them. Few in Blackpool knew that Mrs Augusta Caroline Rosalie Wingfield, who died in her 92nd year on Sunday, had one time been a beauty, a continental toast, who dined with Kings. To the last she remained a Grande Dame who used the best French perfume.

Her last appearance was at the Blackpool Hippodrome [later the ABC Theatre, Church Street. Now demolished], when it was a variety theatre, just before the outbreak of the 1914 war. Since then she had lived quietly at her home in Mere Road.

Her father was Norwegian, her mother German. She was born in Berlin, as a child travelled widely through Russia with her father's circus. Later, near Moscow, when she was a star, her sleigh was attacked on one occasion by wolves.

She became famous in Europe and Asia, topping the bill in Moscow, Kiev, the Moulin Rouge and the Folies Bergere in Paris. In America she was widely known. In England she played at the Crystal Palace and the Alhambra in London, in Blackpool appeared at the Tower, Winter Gardens and the now vanished [Royal Palace Gardens at] Raikes Hall."

The African Blondin - Prince of the Air (1850-1889)

[Charles Trower]

It is reported that Charles Trower was born in the USA but no documents seem to support this. His birth year of 1850 is also questioned, but this date does appear on his marriage and death certificates. He was a very popular and well known black performer in the late Victorian period and appeared at many venues across the United Kingdom and the United States. He was supposedly trained by the great high-wire performer Charles Blondin, but that fact is disputed and the original Blondin did take legal action against the African Blondin for trading on his more famous name. His story is a sad one as he died at the age of 40, from the effects of syphilis, in London. He left a widow and three children. His performances at the Royal Palace Gardens in Blackpool were hugely popular and he always drew great crowds who marvelled at his high-wire exploits.

More information can be found on his family website at:

http://theafricanblondin.com/

Charles Blondin - King of the High-Wire (1824-1897)

Blondin was born on 28 February 1824 at St Omer, Pas-de-Calais, France. His real name was Jean-François Gravelet and he was known also by the names Charles Blondin, Jean-François Blondin and called the "Chevalier Blondin", or simply "The Great Blondin". At the age of five he was sent to the École de Gymnase at Lyon and, after six months training as an acrobat, made his first public appearance as "The boy Wonder". His superior skill and grace, as well as the originality of the settings of his acts, made him a popular favourite. He first married Marie Blancherie, and at the same time legitimised their son Aime Leopold. It is not known what happened to his French family after he went to America.

In 1861, Blondin first appeared in London, at the Crystal Palace, turning somersaults on stilts on a rope stretched across the central transept, 70 feet (20 m) from the ground. In 1862, he again gave a series of performances at the Crystal Palace, and elsewhere in England, and on the continent of Europe. In September 1861 he performed in Edinburgh, Scotland at the Royal Botanic Gardens (then called the Experimental Gardens) on Inverleith Row.

In 1861, he performed at the Royal Portobello Gardens, Dublin, on a rope 50 feet above the ground. While he was performing, the rope broke, which led to the scaffolding collapsing. He was not injured, but two workers who were on the scaffolding fell to their deaths. An investigation was held, and the broken rope (2 inches in diameter and 5 inches in circumference) examined. No blame was attributed at the time to either Blondin or his manager. However, the judge said that the rope manufacturer had a lot to answer for. The organiser of the event, a Mr. Kirby, said he would never have another one like it. A bench warrant for the arrest of Blondin and his manager was issued when they did not appear at a further trial (they were in America). However, the following year, Blondin was back at the same venue in Dublin, this time performing 100 feet above the ground.

He appeared at the Royal Palace Gardens on at least two occasions, thrilling the expectant crowds. His famous feat of crossing Niagara Falls on a rope added to his allure at the gardens.

Leotard Bosco (Raconteur) (1850 - 1895)

When he died at the relatively young age of 45, in July 1895 from diabetes, Leotard Bosco "a dark, dapper little man"[1] was a someone who would be much lamented by his many friends and admirers, according to the fulsome obituary provided in The Stage newspaper. Born with the surname Greethead in 1850 at Bristol, Bosco would start at the very bottom of the theatrical profession as a programme seller at a circus, before learning the art of conjuring from around 1866 and touring with this act before a move into production and theatre management with varying degrees of success for the rest of his life - his last management position being at the Theatre Royal in Aston from where he became very popular "not only with habitués of the theatre but by all those he came into contact with"[2].

John Cooper (Lion Tamer) (c.1833 - 1920)

John Cooper lays out his antecedents very clearly in his notice in the Era where he is advertising his involvement with the great American Circus of J W Myer in Hamburg (1873); he happens to mention that in 1865 he had already performed before His Imperial Majesty, the Emperor of all the Russians. Performing with both Elephants and Lions, you could see these dumb creatures perform "Waltzes and Quadrilles" at the Crystal Palace in 1876. Described by a contemporary writer in the 1890's as "one of the most unassuming men"[3] Cooper would have a long and distinguished career travelling and performing with many of the greatest circus of the age and lived in retirement for many years before his death at the age of 87, in Wolverhampton.

---

[1] Hull Daily Mail - 4th October 1912
[2] The Stage - 1st August 1895
[3] The Era - 4th April 1896

Professor Codman (Punch & Judy) (1832 - 1909)

One of the founding members of a Punch and Judy dynasty - the Codmans, this Professor Codman was Norwich born Richard Codman, who started his show on the promenade at Llandudno in 1860 and would eventually tour both the UK and the world with his puppets and very special performing dog, Toby. With his traditional Punch and Judy show, Professor Codman was a perennial presence at seaside venues, showgrounds and pleasure gardens all through the nineteenth and early twentieth century before he died in Wales in 1909 was succeeded by his son and subsequent generations of Professor Codman's even to this present day.

Gus Elen (Prince of Comedians) (1862 - 1940)

Londoner, Augustus (Gus) Elen began his long career on the stage during the 1880's and could be found on the Ramsgate Sands as part of a burnt cork minstrel act. It was when he returned to London we see the beginnings of the "coster" comedian that would define the remainder of his career. Drawing inspiration from the characters he found in the street around him, Gus Elen would be associated with some of the best known songs from the Music Hall stage; numbers such as "It's a great big shame", "'Arf a pint of ale" and "If it wasn't for the 'ouses in between" would become classics that still resonate today. In the early 1930's Pathe captured Gas Elen on film and you can see the extraordinary talent still possessed of a man, who was by then in his seventies. Off the stage, Gus Elen lived a quiet life, undertook charitable work and retired to the South Coast and passed away in 1940. He is buried in Streatham Park Cemetery and his grave is cared for by The Music Hall Guild of Great Britain and America.

Little Valdo and Tom Felix (Clowns)

Billed variously as the "Great Little Clown" and "the unrivalled clown" Little Valdo appears with a satisfying consistency from an appearance at the opening of the Alexandra Palace in 1880 right through to the early twentieth century and particularly associated with the equestrian pantomimes at Covent Garden during the 1880's. As well as traditional clowning, Little Valdo appears with a number of performing "animals" as part of his act including the "Blondin Donkey" and a bogus Elephant. As is typical of the mystique of clowns, it is difficult to uncover who the real Little Valdo was, but he was clearly a competent and successful clown and one of his son's would marry the daughter of the great circus owner Charles Hengler.

With his career beginning in the late 1860's Tom Felix had already established his name by the time he appears on the same bill as Little Valdo in 1880. Born Thomas Mileson in London in 1850, Tom Felix begins a career in clowning that would see him spend much of the latter part of the nineteenth century touring with circus's in Europe, before returning in 1900 and then disappearing once again. A clown of the comic tumbling and acrobatic variety, Tom Felix basks, throughout his career in the glow of positive notices, seemingly blessed, or indeed cursed by the clown's need to always be funny.

Frank Gilfort (High Wire) (c.1850 - 1899)

"The Great American Gladiator" Frank Gilfort arrived in England in 1878 with a high wire act that was meant to emulate the hero of Niagara, Blondin. Certainly he did well to outdo that most famous equilibrist by "walking in chains and standing on his head at the centre of the rope" and on another occasion, "descending from the rope by his teeth", perhaps deservedly earning his new billed name "The American Blondin". The rope being set at 40 feet from the ground and 300 feet long. A little later in his career during the late 1880's, he starts to involve his son and daughter, Annie Gilfort in the act. In 1899 he sustains an injury to his knee cap, which following an amputation, develops into sepsis and he dies at the home of his acrobat brother, Robert in Orange, New Jersey, USA on the 13th March 1899[4]

Glennies Royal Marionettes (Puppet Troupe)

Any details are scare but I did discover that some of the puppets used by this troupe, or a member of it, dated circa. 1880 atill exist. This website has some interesting information for anyone who would like to research this a bit more. Puppet shows were hugely popular in Victorian England, and these Marrionette Troupes toured the country and also the Royal Palace

---

[4] San Francisco Call - 13th March 1899

Gardens in Blackpool. They would act out popular fairy tales or even actual events at the time to the delight of audiences.

https://www.doeandhope.com/products/a-rare-group-of-fifteen-c-1880s-marionettes-from-a-travelling-english-troupe?variant=1253672408

Edgard Granville – Comedian (** - 1909)

A comedian and raconteur who worked the halls and, due to the number of dates and performances across the country, was a popular comedian of his time. He performed at the Royal Palace Gardens in Blackpool at least twice. There is very little information about him but the East London Theatre Archive do have a listing for him in the programme for the Mile End Empire, a popular hall of the day.

http://www.elta-project.org/browse.html?recordId=1711

Mrs. Hunt's Ladies Orchestra. (Popular Music Musicians and Costumed)

This popular ladies orchestra broke some new ground for women – especially performing in public to paying audiences. At the time it was considered a novelty to see an all women orchestra. They also added to the performances by adorning period or historic costumes. Two books are useful for further reading:

Scott, Derek B. Sounds of the Metropolis: The 19th Century Popular Music Revolution. Oxford University Press, UK. 2008. Page 22

John Holturn (Herr Holturn (Holtum) -King of the Cannon) (1845 - 1919) [year of death unverifiable]

From an interview given in the Oxford Journal in 1891[5], Herr Holturn states that he was born in Denmark as John F Haldorson on the 20th October 1845 and ran away to sea, ending up in San Francisco, where following some pecuniary difficulties he aspired to a stage career and began balancing chairs and juggling with bottles. He joined a circus and eventually found himself in New York, where he had the idea of catching a cannon ball fired from a cannon. It was only when he arrived in England that the cannon was manufactured and he commenced a European Tour, with Charles Hengler's Circus. Later he would issue a challenge to see if anyone could catch the ball themselves, which in turn saw him arrested in Leeds following an injury sustained by a contestant. Ever the true showman and following his acquittal Herr Holtum, turned this misfortune into a great piece of publicity attracting huge crowds to his show of strength and extraordinary bravery.

Miss Katie Laurence (Serio Comic and Vocalist) (1866 – 1913)

Defined by her most famous song "Daisy Bell", written by Harry Dacre in 1892, Katie Lawrence enjoyed a successful career as a serio vocalist with a wider repertoire of songs than is ever remembered. The daughter of a veterinary surgeon, Emily Elizabeth Guppy was born in London 1866 and is first seen on the stage in 1883, billed as a serio and dancer. A prolific performer Katie Lawrence capitalised on her "Daisy Bell" success would be regarded as a leading Music Hall and principal pantomime performer during the next twenty years - appearing across the UK and overseas in the major territories of the British Empire. She was married twice, first to agent George Fuller in 1888 and following his death in 1909, to Reginald Gervase in 1910. Sadly, only a few years later, in 1913, Katie Lawrence passed away at Birmingham at the young age of only 44.

Professor Charles Morritt – Magician & Hypnotist (1860-1936)

Morritt was a magician and stage hypnotist who was born in Saxton, Yorkshire. He performed all over the country and appeared at the City Variety in Leeds and in many pleasure gardens including Blackpool's Royal Palace Gardens. He is credited for creating several magic tricks including The Flying Lady that her performed with the help of his wife at Blackpool.

---

[5] Oxford Journal - 3rd October 1891

Sadly he turned to drink and ended up down at heel. He was accused of fraud with one trick and he always insisted on his innocence – the charges were later dropped.

More information at:

http://freepages.history.rootsweb.ancestry.com/~calderdalecompanion/mmm167.html

Harry Rogerson (Comedian) (1872 – 1952)

Born in Lincoln in 1872, Harry Rogerson followed his father, comic actor Whit Rogerson onto the stage and makes his first recorded appearance in 1893 in the burlesque "Madcap Mavis" at the Comedy Theatre, Manchester. A long and successful career followed in pantomime and on the Music Hall stage as a comedian, before Harry Rogerson expands into production and company management at the turn of the century. This was combined with continued stage work and comic writing until 1930 when he retired. He was married to actress Bessie Heath in 1895 and they had 3 children together - he died in Brighton in 1952.

Saville Swallow Orchestra (1840 - 1903)

Born in Ashton, Lancashire in 1840, the exotically named Saville Swallow is first seen in musical circles as a pianist in 1865 at the Ardwick Glee Club. Two years later he is loosely associated with **other "instrumentalists" and by 1874 he is regarded as a** Professor of Music, acting as a judge for music competitions held at temperance halls in and around the North West of England. It was in 1875 that we find him playing at a high profile wedding in Bakewell and first billed as Saville Swallow's Quadrille Band. Clearly a talented pianist and highly competent musician, Swallow died in Manchester in 1903 and was considered, according to the Burnley Times in 1930, as "little if at all inferior to Mr Halle"[6]

---

[6] Burnley News - 19th July 1903

Mark Sheridan (Comedian) (1867 – 1918)

Hailing from County Durham, Mark Sheridan was born as Fred Shaw and started his performing career as a double act "The Sheridans". As a solo turn he appeared dressed eccentrically in his trademark high top hat and bell bottom trousers and with a huge repertoire of very popular chorus songs that included "I do like to be beside the seaside" and "Here we are again" - Mark Sheridan was in the very front rank of Music Hall comedians. With his wife and son, Mark Sheridan toured with a burlesque company during the first world war before falling under the mistaken impression that his popularity was waning and tragically taking a gun to himself in Glasgow in 1918.

Miss Bertie Stokes (Ballads) (c.1854 - 1898)

Making her first recorded debut in Wolverhampton in 1868; soprano and descriptive Vocalist, Miss Bertie Stokes (Theresa Bertha Jones) goes on to be a popular performer for the next 30 years. Known principally as a singer of popular songs, Bertie Stokes had a wide repertoire and during the 1870's was also proving very popular with the "Male Impersonation" part of her act. She would be married to the impressionist George Medley in 1883 and they could be seen on the same bill from the late 1880's onwards - sadly, he would die at the young age of 44 in 1898 with his widow receiving the financial assistance of her theatrical confreres in the shape of a benefit held at the London Pavilion, this **event marking the apparent end of her career. In 1900 she marries Solicitor William Bull, living in** apparent comfort until her death, at Mitcham, at the age of 85 in 1939.

Miss Nellie Stratton (Comic and Dancer) (1875 - 1947)

First coming to the attention of the public in 1890, Nellie Stratton begins her career performing in light musical comedy productions before developing a Music Hall turn in her own right and performing successfully on the syndicate circuit and annually in pantomime for the next twenty years. She married Comedian Wilkie Bard in 1895 and later in her career she appeared in her husband's revue productions and they celebrated their silver wedding anniversary in 1920.

(J.A. Whelan Balloonist)

Whelan, known as 'the people's William' was a popular balloonist and stunt artist in the late Victorian period. He appeared more than once at the Royal Palace Gardens and always drew large, excited crowds to witness the wonderful technology of flight. He had an acrobat who would leap from the balloon at height and attached to a rope and harness. This would draw large gasps of excitement from the crowds gathered below. This could be an early version of bungee jumping!

Johnny Whiteman (Comic) (1865 - 1937)

Born in Pontefract in 1865, John C (Johnny) Whiteman would have a long and varied theatrical career. In 1888, Johnny Whiteman would be seen in his local theatre as Sarah the Cook in the annual pantomime. After a short stint on the stage as a comic singer and having a big hit with the song "Phil the Fluter's Ball" he would go on to be the acting manager at the famous City Varieties in Leeds remaining involved with the same hall for over four decades before joining his brother Albert Whiteman in his agency and taking over fully during the late 1920's. He was a well-liked and popular figure in the North of England and was known for helping young performers take their first steps in the Variety world. He married in 1895, had two children and died in Leeds in 1937.

Index

A
ABC Theatre. 2
Afghan War. 49
African Blondin. 50,52,53,85,137,140
Albin, Monsieur. 64,137
Alivanti, King of Loose Wire. 67,137
Allens, Charles. Circus. 72,139
Alice & Dr. Beauclere. Magic. 78
Ayton, George. 78

B
Banks, Thomas Lewis. 30,31
Bampton, Rev. George. 23
Bamber, Mr. 118,121
Barnum & Bailey Circus. 123
Barry, Adrian. 1
Barrs Flying Hawks. 50,137
Basutos. 125
Belle Vue [Strawberry Gardens]. 9,34,35,46,47, 69,72,76,83,97,105
Beristor Acrobats. 78
Bickerstaff, Sir John. 105,106,130
Bikee Taylor's Comic Opera. 138
Bishop Goss of Liverpool. 17,19
Blacker, Dave MBE. 5
Blondin. 61,85,95,100,101,127,138,141
Boer War. 121,122
Bosco, Leotard. 62,137,142
Bradley, Charley. 119
Bridges, Mother Mary Ignatia. 19,21
Brookes, G.H. 122
Brown, Sir Samuel. 52,54
Bruce, Robert T. 50,54,59
Burch, William. 29
Butcher, James. 47
Butcher [Bucher], William. 8,11,12,13,14,17,25

C
Carr, James. 17
Cardwell, James. 31
Castle Gardens [Carlton] 77
Cassie, Charles. 138
Central Pier. 16
Chapman, Walter. 48
Christiano, Ed. i, 3
Churchill, Winston. 5
Claremont Park. 29
Clark, Pamela. 78
Clemence, Lloyd. 72
Clifton Hotel. 96
Cocker Street Baths. 97
Codman, Professor. 72,138,143
Coliseum. 96
Connelly, Cornelia. 15,16,17,18,19,20,21, 22,23,24,27,135
Connelly, Piere. 20,21
Conway, Miss. 138
Cooper, John. 67,137,142
Cookson, Richard. 16
Crime, John. 29
Crystal Palace. 31,96,106

E
Eldred, William. 126
Elen, Gus. 98,138,143
Essman, Monsiour. 93
Exley, Charles. 59
Eyre, Kathleen. 12,135

F
Felix, Tom. 67
Fernandez Trio [Acrobats]. 72,138
Fish, John. 30,36,37,49,52,54
Fisher, Henry. 29
Fillis, Frank. 122,125,126
Fillis, Madame. 125
Fowler, Ebeneezer. 29
Fowler, Captain. 98,138
Fox Hall. 13,25
Frazell, Nellie. 99,138

G
Gerritis Clowns. 138
Gilfort, John Frank. 70,137,144
Glennies Marionettes. 78,138,144
Glover, John Holmes. 70
Gordon, Nora. 138
Gosling & Wright. 61,137
Granville, Edgar. 138,145
Grundy, Thomas. 62
Guvnor Company. 72

H
Hanson, Mother Theresa. 16
Hanson, Sir Reginals. 79
Hardacre, J Pitt. 122
Harper, Charles. 119
Harvey, Charley. 138
Harvey, Rose. 138
Hawks, Sarah. 48
Hector & Victor Acrobats. 76
Hengler's Circus. 70,139
King Henry VIII. 26
Hoffman, Herr. 83
Higgins, Mother Mary. 23
Hippodrome Theatre. 2
Hodgson, John. 34,46,48,69,83
Holland, William. 87,101
Holtum, John. 64,98,137,138,146
Hornby, Daniel. 14
Hornby Family. 8,23
Hornby, William. 14,18
Howard, James. 29
Howard, Professor. 100,106,107
Hunt, Maggie. 70,137
Hunt Orchestra. 138,145

151

D
Day, Mother Gretrude. 24
Deeper Blue Designs. i, 3
Denamoes High Wire. 138
DeVere, C. Magician. 78,138
Dexter, Professor. 82
Didsbury Hotel [No 3]. 29,46,48

K
Kay, Alphonsa. 16
Kitchener, Lord. 124
Kruger, President. 123

L
Laurence, Katie. 93,138,146
Latvo Sisters. 70,137
Lennox, Lottie. 138
Leglere Acrobats. 138
Lilo, Elspa & Echo [Trapeze] 78,138
Lomax & Sons. 90
Lloyd, Gracie. 138

M
McLaughlin, John Cameron. 127,129
Mitchell, Thomas. 59
Montanas Magic Act. 138
Morrit, Professor. 100,138,147
Music Hall Guild of GB. i
Mycock, Thomas. 35
Myers Great American Circus. 57,64,66,67,136,139
Myers, M. Coroner. 26
Myer, Rose. 67,137

N
Nasrullah, Prince. 99
Neil, Matthew. i
Nemo, Mr. 36,41,42,48,49,52,53,76
North Pier. 29,31,32,69,96

O
Oxford Hotel. 97
Oxford Music Hall, London. 70
Oxford Pleasure Grounds. 77

P
Pango/Man Monkey. 78
Palmer, Little Daisy. 138
Parkinson, Jacob. 31.
Paton, Sir Noel. 92
Pietro, Father de. 19
Phillipataoux. 61, 97
Plimpton Roller Skates. 38,46
Pomona Gardens. 30
Powell, Baden. 123,124
Preston Guardian. 26
Price, Benjamin. 101
Prince of Wales Theatre. 97

Q
Queens Theatre [prev Feldmans]. 97

I
Illuminations. 89
Iddeson, Charles. 91,93,97,98,106,118,121

J
Jackson, Peter. 19
Jones, William Thomas VC. 78

S
Sagrino. 67
Salvation Army Citadel. 34,120
Savage South Africa. 122,123,124,125,127,136,139
Saville Swallow Orchestra. 48,61,137
Seddon, Alan. Ii, 1
St Johns Church.29
Shrewsbury, Lord. 20
Shuter, Mr. [Gardener]. 36,37,38,40
Shultz, Herr. 67

Signor, Capra. 125
Simecourt, Marie. 93,138
Sheridan, Mark. 100,138,148
Silbow Troupe. 48,49
Sisters of the Holy Child Jesus. 15,21,23
Smith, Joseph. 29,45
South Pier. 32,96
Stansfield, Mr. 81,82
Stokes, Bertie. 70,137,148
Stratton, Nellie. 100,138,148

T
Talbot Hotel. 20
Tannacker, Mr. 8,81
Taylor, George Bart. 70,77,87,88,89 ,91
Theatre Royal. 97
Trainor, Christopher. 101
Thornton, Alice. 16,21,22
Thornber, William. 11,12
Tivoli Gardens. 7,129
Tivoli Theatre, Strand, London. 134
Trochene Horses. 67
Tower. 7,11,98,105
Turpin, Dick. 70
Tyldesly Family. 25

V
Valdo, Little & Felix, Tom. 67,137,143
Valmore, Jenny. 93,134,138
Vatican. 96
Velones Acrobats. 93
Queen Victoria. 1,78,79,118,119,124
Viener, Adolf Moritz. 29,45
Visser, Pier. 124

W
Walton, John. 33

R
Raikes Hall Guards. 48
Railway Hotel. 16
Ramsden, Harry. 96
Rastus Flying Man. 63,137
Read, Enoch. 88
Read, Jonathan. 29,30,70,71
Reads Baths. 97
Regent Cinema. 2
Rhodes, Cecil. 99
Riding, Elijah. 3
Rogerson, Harry. 138,147
Rose, Alphonsine La Belle. 54,55,75,139
Rowbone, Captain Loxton. 91
Rushton, Ralph. 30

Ward, Jennie Ann. 88
Ward, Peter. 91
Watson, Tom. 67
Westminster Abbey. 96
Whelan, Captain JA. 62,65,87,137,149
Whiteman, Johny. 138
Whitley, John. 87,149
Winter Gardens. 7,11,59,69,87,97,98,101,105
Wood, Flo. 138
Worthington, Thomas Parkinson. 30

Z
Zagro Sisters. 70,137
Zoro Equibrilist. 70,137

David Slattery-Christy - 2016

Other books available by this author:

In Search of Ruitania: The Life & Times of Ivor Novello
Anything But Merry: The Life & Times of Lily Elsie
Mildred On The Marne: Mildred Aldrich Frontline Witness 1914-1918
Edwardian Beauty – Lily Elsie & The Merry Widow
The Mistletoe Haunting – Legend of Minster Lovell

Plays

Elvira & I – Puccini's Scandalous Passions!
Forever Nineteen
The Post Card
After The Tone

Libretto

Glamorous Night – A Musical Play
By Ivor Novello & Christopher Hassall –
Revised Book & Lyrics David Slattery-Christy

ABOUT THE AUTHOR

David Slattery-Christy is an award-winning playwright and author. His new novel The Mistletoe Haunting - Legend of Minster Lovell released 26 February 2016: "A beautiful book, and beautifully written." Kat Orman, BBC Radio Oxford 22/1/16 ***Author and his Novello biography 'In Search of Ruritania' Featured on BBC Radio 2 documentary on Ivor Novello with Don Black titled: Keep The Home Fires Burning as part of the BBC Great War Centenary broadcasts. *** Soon to be featured on the BBC Radio 3 'Composer of the Week' programme dedicated to Ivor Novello.

David was born in Oxford, England, in 1959. He graduated from London's City University with a BA (Hons) Degree in Journalism. In addition to this he has a Teaching Degree from Lancaster University and a Masters Degree in the Arts from the University of Central Lancashire and continues his professional development by undertaking research and history courses at the University of Oxford. Prior to this he attended London Theatre Arts to study drama, and then worked extensively in the performing arts industry as a playwright, producer and director. His stage plays include the award winning Forever Nineteen, After The Tone and The Post Card - which enjoyed London and New York productions, as well as touring nationally in the United Kingdom. His involvement in adapting the libretto for Ivor Novello's 1935 musical Glamorous Night resulted in him directing the 50th Anniversary Concert to celebrate the life and work of Novello at the Theatre Royal, Drury Lane, in London's West End. Subsequently he has worked as the Ivor Novello Consultant on Julian Fellowes and Robert Altman's Oscar and BAFTA winning film Gosford Park, and contributed to the BBC Documentary on the life of Novello The Handsomest Man in Britain. He is the author of In Search of Ruritania, a biography on Ivor Novello - Anything But Merry! The Life and Times of Lily Elsie the Edwardian actress and singer who found fame in Lehar's The Merry Widow; the novel based on the legend of a mistletoe bride titled The Mistletoe Haunting: Legend of Minster Lovell and a WW1 biography Mildred on the Marne: Mildred Aldrich, Front-line Witness 1914-1918. Currently he is developing a play based on the relationship between opera composer Puccini and his wife, Elvira.

Further information available at: www.christyplays.com

Royal Palace Gardens

Printed in Poland
by Amazon Fulfillment
Poland Sp. z o.o., Wrocław